Tales from the Wake Forest Hardwood

Dan Collins

Foreword by Skip Prosser

www.SportsPublishingLLC.com

ISBN: 1-58261-746-5

Publisher: Peter L. Bannon
Senior managing editor: Susan M. Moyer
Acquisitions editor: Mike Pearson
Developmental editor: Doug Hoepker
Dust jacket design: Kenneth J. O'Brien
Project manager: Alicia Wentworth
Imaging: Dustin Hubbart, Heidi Norsen, Kenneth J. O'Brien
Copy editor: Cynthia L. McNew
Photo editor: Erin Linden-Levy
Vice president of sales and marketing: Kevin King
Media and promotions managers: Kelley Brown (regional),
        Randy Fouts (national), Maurey Williamson (print)

Printed in the United States of America

Sports Publishing L.L.C.
804 North Neil Street
Champaign, IL 61820

Phone: 1-877-424-2665
Fax: 217-363-2073
Web site: www.SportsPublishingLLC.com

To Skeeter Francis,
who saw it all—and then some.

Contents

Foreword

When one thinks of Wake Forest basketball it is quite easy to conjure up names such as Murray Greason, Bones McKinney, Len Chappell, "Muggsy" Bogues, and Tim Duncan. Around Winston-Salem and the state of North Carolina, the name of Dan Collins is synonymous with Wake Forest basketball.

Since coming to Wake Forest I have come to know of the abiding love Demon Deacons have for their basketball. Graduates of "Old Wake Forest" in Wake County are united in this love with more recent graduates of the picturesque newer campus in Winston-Salem. It is also amazing how many die-hard Wake fans are not graduates, but simply those who appreciate the unique combination found at Wake of strong academics and winning basketball. This marriage of high graduation rates and basketball victories has made the legions of Wake Forest fans justly proud of their school and their team.

I have come to know Dan very well in the three years I have been at Wake Forest. Dan has always proven to be conscientious and professional. Born and raised in ACC basketball country, Dan's love for the game and appreciation for its history is readily apparent in his writing. Dan also has shown an amazing talent for finding the story "behind" the story.

In the pages of this book Dan Collins brings the rich tradition and love of Wake Forest basketball to life. Dan reveals a history that sees Wake Forest play the first college game in North Carolina. From colorful coaches to championship teams, Dan weaves a tale rich with color and tradition. Demon Deacon fans will love this tribute to Wake Forest basketball as much as they love the university and her team.

—Skip Prosser
Wake Forest Basketball Head Coach

Acknowledgments

A warm and heartfelt thanks to the following, without whose support, assistance and friendship this book could have never been written: Gary Strickland; Julie Griffin; Dean Buchan and his staff at the Wake Forest sports information department, in particular Leslie Short for helping with the photographs; sports editor Terry Oberle and the rest of the sports staff at the *Winston-Salem Journal*; Maurice George; Billy Packer; Richard Carmichael; Susan Brinkley; Murray Greason, Jr.; Carl Tacy; Abe Elmore; Jackie Murdock; Charlie Bryant; John Justus; Jody Puckett; Coach Skip Prosser and his staff of the Wake Forest basketball program, in particular Lynne Heflin and Mary Ann Justus; David Zucchino; editor Doug Hoepker; and the three most special people of my world, Tybee, Nate and Rebecca.

Prologue

The Newark Airport, gritty and gray as I remembered it from my last time through, some years ago, is practically deserted early Saturday afternoon. As I subject myself to security, slipping off my belt and shoes, digging the coins and keys from my pocket, a sudden realization as warm and healing as a Carolina morning in April all but bowls me over.

"Last time I'll be doing this 'til football season," I mention to the visibly bored man passing my belongings beneath the scanner. "I'm heading home."

For five and half months I followed the bouncing ball, until the ball I was following stopped bouncing around midnight two nights before at the Continental Airlines Arena, about 15 miles north via the New Jersey Turnpike. The headlong pursuit in four-minute media timeout increments ended when the Wake Forest Deacons, the college basketball team I've covered now for a dozen years for the hometown newspaper, the *Winston-Salem Journal*, lost to St. Joseph's 84-80 in the semifinals of the East Rutherford Regional.

"Wake Forest's season reached a bitter end at the Sweet 16" I dashed off in the 30 minutes allotted before crushing deadline considerations required my story be in the hands of my editors 500 miles south.

"We had a great team this year," the Deacons' freshmen sensation Chris Paul said. "A lot of people talk about us being good next year, but we thought we could make a run deep in the tournament this year.

"So it's tough to know that the season's over."

Paul and his teammates had dreamed of a trip the next weekend to San Antonio and the Final Four, and I had hoped to be along. San Antonio, as I found at the Final Four of 1998, is a great town. Austin, only an hour away, is even better, my favorite town of all not located in North Carolina. Even more compelling, though, was the story I was writing of a young team that grew up right before my eyes over a forced march through the ACC season into the NCAA Tournament.

The Deacons, seeded fourth after finishing the regular season with a 19-9 record, met the NCAA Tournament's expectations by being one of the final 16 teams still in the hunt for a national crown. Their own sights had been set higher, however, and they fought hard to keep alive their dream of being the first Wake Forest team to reach the Final Four since 1962.

Scoring 12 points in the last 1:14 of their season, they sliced all but two points off an eight-point St. Joseph's lead. After Justin Gray's driving basket with 12 seconds left closed the gap to 82-80 they trapped Jameer Nelson, the Hawks' All-America guard, in the corner, clawing desperately at the ball.

But Nelson managed to heave the ball ahead to Delonte West, his backcourt running mate and West, an 88-percent free throw shooter, dropped in both of his fouls shots with just 6.4 seconds remaining.

So St. Joseph's sent Wake Forest home, with an admonition for any team that happens to end up across an NCAA Tournament bracket from the Deacons in seasons to come. Even after the decision of freshman Todd Hendley to transfer to UNC Wilmington, 11 of the 12 players on scholarship were eligible to return for the 2004-05 season. Paul, who was everything he was expected to be as a freshman, and more, appeared to be just the player to lead the Deacons to the Promised Land.

"Anybody that doesn't think that team is going to contend for the national championship as long as Chris Paul is in school, you've lost your mind," was the unsolicited opinion of Phil Martelli, St. Joseph's city-wise coach. "That team will be right in the mix next year and the year after, as long as that kid stays in school."

Coach Skip Prosser of the Deacons bore up under the disappointment as best he could. Prosser, as those who know him best will attest, takes losing hard.

Sitting on the podium, addressing the media still hanging around for the latest of the late games, he was able to look past the disappointment of the moment into a bright future.

"We're trying to do something at Wake Forest," Prosser said. "As Churchill would say, it's not the end; the end is just the beginning. In terms of scholarship players, we have all these kids back.

"We're just looking forward to getting to the point where we have a hard-core veteran leadership-type group, and we're getting there."

As I look up from my laptop, 38 hours later, I notice that Gate 37 of the Newark Airport has gotten busier. An agent picks up a microphone to announce that Flight 1203 to Charlotte International is getting ready to board.

I'm heading home.

—Dan Collins

Chapter 1

The Pre-ACC Years

In the Beginning

A man from Indiana named Everett Case was credited for bringing big-time basketball to North Carolina when he was hired to coach at N.C. State in the halcyon days just after World War II.

There was another man from Indiana, however, who actually brought the game itself to Wake Forest four decades earlier.

Richard Crozier, born in Evansville, migrated south to Wake County, N.C. in the spring of 1904 to coach the Wake Forest baseball team. A year later, having been named director of the campus gymnasium, Crozier introduced basketball to the student body. A year after that, in 1906, he held tryouts for Wake Forest's first intercollegiate team.

The game was in its infancy, having been invented only 15 years earlier by James Naismith at what today is called Springfield College in Springfield, Massachusetts.

The seven players chosen for Wake Forest's first team were V.F. (Vanderbilt) Crouch, team captain, O.W. (Oscar) Ward, Kyle Elliott, T.H. Beverly, Earl Gore, B.F. Keith and J.B. (James)

Turner. Crouch and Ward were listed as forwards, Elliott, at a towering 6-5, was the center, and Beverly and Gore started in the backcourt. Keith and Turner were reserves.

In an interview with Tom Bost printed by the *Raleigh News and Observer* on March 2, 1952, Crozier explained that the game of basketball was still a few decades away from the slam dunks, drop steps and cross-over dribbles of today.

"Basketball in those days was a very rough and strenuous game," Crozier said. "Few fouls were called, 10 or 12 being about the average called on one team the whole game. Close guarding was allowed and you had to pass or shoot at the goal very quickly, else the guard was all over you tussling for possession of the ball. That made the defense more effective, and incidentally cut down scoring—goals were just harder to get. If the same style of defense was allowed today, I believe it would cut down the scoring quite a lot. However, I would say that while there was not more scoring in the old game, believe me when I say, there was plenty of action."

Crozier's team specialized in the passing game and the fast break. Drawing on his earlier experiences, he taught the baseball pass.

"Every man on the squad could rifle the ball full length of the floor with the same accuracy that a catcher in baseball throws to second base," Crozier said. "My theory was 'Why make a half-dozen or more passes to get the ball down the floor when two or three would do the work and quicker?'"

Crozier apparently knew his stuff. In 12 seasons as Wake Forest's head coach, his teams won 95 games and lost 46 and never suffered a losing season.

Shrouded in Time

It has been firmly established that Wake Forest first played intercollegiate basketball in 1906. It has been established that the first team, known quite appropriately as the Baptists, won three games and lost three. And it has also been established that the Baptists played the first game of intercollegiate basketball ever in the state of North Carolina.

But lost in the fog of time are who exactly the Deacons played the first game against, and whether they won or lost.

Certain historical accounts recorded that Wake Forest played the first game against Guilford on February 6, 1906 on the first leg of a four-game road trip against the Quakers, the Charlotte YMCA, the Spartanburg YMCA and Wofford College. If so, then the Baptists lost their first game to the Quakers by a score of 26-19.

But Crozier remembered it differently. In a letter to Marvin "Skeeter" Francis, Wake Forest's sports information director, Crozier wrote that the Baptists actually played their first game against Trinity, a school now known as Duke.

Crozier's letter, dated June 18, 1961, was written from his home in Greenville, S.C.

"I introduced basketball at Wake Forest in 1906," Crozier wrote. "We played the first intercollegiate game ever to be played in North Carolina against Trinity."

If Crozier's memory served him well, the Baptists won their first game, beating Trinity 15-5 in Wake Forest's only home game of the season. They swept the series against Trinity, winning 24-10 in Durham.

The best evidence that Crozier's recollection was off comes from the *Wake Forest Weekly*, the campus newspaper, which reported that the Baptists played at Trinity on March 2, and at home against Trinity on March 14. But to further shroud the issue, the *Wake Forest Weekly* referred to the game at Trinity as the second intercollegiate game played in the state of North Carolina.

The Baptists of 1906, Wake Forest's first basketball team. (Courtesy of Wake Forest Media Relations)

If Wake Forest made a four-game road trip earlier, then the Baptists would have presumably played two previous games in North Carolina, at Guilford and at Charlotte. That is, unless they played the Charlotte YMCA in a tournament held in the state of South Carolina.

What seems clear is that the game made an immediate splash at Wake Forest, as the account from the *Wake Forest Weekly* of the Baptists' 15-5 victory over Trinity revealed.

"In a hotly contested game Wake Forest again defeated Trinity," the author wrote. "The game was pulled off in the gymnasium at Wake Forest, and was seen by a large crowd of spectators, who were kept at the highest pitch of excitement by playing on both sides."

Something to Brag About

From the earliest days college hoops were played in North Carolina, Wake Forest took immense pride in its basketball team. The 1907 squad, the second the college ever fielded, established early bragging rights with 4-0 record. The Baptists outscored their opponents that season 110-24, and held two opponents without a field goal.

One of the victims, it should be noted, was a high school team from Littleton. The older, more physically mature college athletes drubbed the school kids 53-6. But hey, competition was hard to find in those days.

The 1906 edition of *The Howler*, the Wake Forest yearbook, supplied no written account of the school's first basketball team, but did provide a picture of Crozier and his team, which won three games and lost three.

By 1907, however, the sport had become enough of a buzz on campus that *The Howler* waxed poetic over the masterwork of its basketball team.

"This year marks the closing of our second season of inter-collegiate basket-ball," began the text. "To say that we had a good team is putting it mildly; to say that we had the best team in the state is more nearly the truth, though that is perhaps not enough.

"From a good team last year, the first put out by Wake Forest, we have developed an aggregation that is easily the best team in the state."

The nucleus of the team was four returnees from the year before, captain Vanderbilt Couch, center Kyle Elliott (a 6-5 giant who towered over his times), and guards T.H. Beverly and James Turner. It should come as no surprise that Couch, Beverly and Turner also played baseball at Wake Forest, given that Crozier also coached the Baptist nine.

Beverly, the text reveals, was the first swingman to play for Wake Forest, the forerunner to the likes of Marc Blucas, Josh Howard and Trent Strickland.

"Beverly alternated between forward and guard," *The Howler* proclaimed, "doing fine work in both places."

The passage ended with an example of early 20th Century trash-talking.

"Mr. Crozier has made an enviable reputation as a coach," *The Howler* proclaimed. "He issued a challenge to any team in the South, which none of them saw fit to accept, however."

"Basketball is Our Game"

W hen Skip Prosser became head coach at Wake Forest before the 2001-02 season, he immediately began a campaign to liven the atmosphere at the Deacons' home games.

"I was told before I took this job," Prosser said many times, "that Wake Forest is not a hard place to play."

Though he wouldn't be expected to know it, Prosser was only attempting to rekindle the passion and excitement that has surrounded Wake Forest basketball since the earliest days.

From 1896 through 1907, Wake Forest did not field a football team.

In March of 1907, a reporter for the student newspaper, the *Wake Forest Student*, wrote, "Basketball is our game—our substitute for football."

Two years later, after the Baptists finished 6-1, a student didn't even attempt to mask his enthusiasm.

"First the team is invincible," read a letter to the newspaper. "We have never lost a game on our floor and this year's team is better than any we fans boast in the history over basket-ball at Wake Forest."

By 1910, *The Howler* described the hoops fever that inflicted the school.

"No department of college athletics receives more hearty support at WF than basketball," proclaimed the yearbook. "The gymnasium is crowded at every game, with plenty of enthusiasm on the side line and a winning team on the floor."

By 1913, according to the *Raleigh News and Observer*, the sport was such a sensation that a home game against Emory and Henry drew 500 spectators.

Nine Years in Decline

By the time Wall Street crashed in 1929, Wake Forest was already one year into an equally sudden, if not as universally calamitous and devastating, decline in fortunes that would sink the once-proud basketball program into a deep nine-year depression.

The Deacons of 1927, under first-year coach James Baldwin, won 22 and lost only three while sporting an 11-1 record against in-state rivals. They won two games against rival N.C. State, including a 20-18 victory witnessed by the largest crowd ever assembled to date at the Wake Forest gymnasium.

A high-powered offensive juggernaut, they featured the top three scorers in the state of North Carolina. Al Dowtin scored 271 points, Ralph James scored 240 and Fred "Cowboy" Emmerson scored 187.

"The big thing on offense was fake, dribble and shoot," James recalled. "But the game was defense. You were permitted to play strong defense and the players who went for the basket were considered on their own."

The 1928 season began well enough, when Wake Forest beat the Raleigh YMCA 45-29. Then back-to-back losses to the Red Terrors of N.C. State triggered an eight-game losing streak that sent the Deacons spiraling to a 6-14 record.

Not until 1937 did Wake Forest manage another winning season. During those nine years of destitution, the Deacons were coached by five different men, Baldwin, Pat Miller, R.S.

Hayes, Emmerson and Murray Greason. They won 50 games and lost 92.

Three developments pulled the Deacons from the doldrums.

In 1934 Wake Forest hired Greason, who, despite three losing seasons, proved to be as adept a coach as he was a star athlete a decade earlier.

Construction of Gore Gym began in 1933 and the facility, named for alumnus and benefactor Claude Gore, opened in the spring of 1935. With a capacity of 2,200, it was considered a showplace for its time.

And in 1936 Wake Forest joined the Southern Conference.

Thus there was great excitement in the air when the 1937 Deacons roared out to a 6-1 start, weathered back-to-back losses to N.C. State and George Washington and won five of their last six to finish 15-6.

At Wake Forest, it could be said that happy days were clearly here again. The Deacons, after slipping to 7-12 in 1938, won the Southern Conference regular-season championships in 1939 and finished 18-6 overall.

"It Was Wild"

To know what Gore Gym was like, you really had to be there. And from the time Gore opened during the spring of 1935 until Wake Forest moved to Winston-Salem in the summer of 1956, few people were there more often than Murray Greason, Jr.

"It was a wonderful place," Greason said.

Gore Gym was one year old when Greason was born not many miles away. Greason's father, Murray Greason, had been head basketball coach at Wake Forest for two seasons.

So the setting of Greason's childhood was, for the most part, Wake Forest's 2,200-seat basketball arena.

"It was wild," Greason Jr. said of Gore. "You take the wildest thing you could see when everybody is revved up at Joel Coliseum, and you compress it into this little box.

"There was always a contest between the volunteer fire chief and people who wanted to get in there, because there was a limit that they tried to enforce. But I am satisfied that on a number of occasions that limit got violated."

Gore Gym was indeed a gym. The Deacons practiced there, so there were no permanent seats. Bleachers were hauled in from the football stadium for home games.

The court measured only 90 feet end to end, instead of the standard 94 feet. The benches were along the baseline, and visiting players invariably found themselves sitting directly in front of members of the Wake Forest football team.

"There were about six risers of bleachers and the football team would customarily get there early enough to sit right behind the benches and harass them," Greason, Jr. said. "There were stories about guys having the hair on their legs pulled when they were trying to take the ball out of bounds."

Jackie Murdock, a star guard from 1955 through 1957, recalled having to stand between the legs of his English professor, Dr. Ed Wilson, to throw the ball inbounds. The faculty customarily sat on the front row.

"I said, if we win this game, I won't be in class tomorrow," Murdock said. "And all the faculty laughed at him.

"The next morning he came into class, and the first thing he did was look over there and see if I was there.

"I was there."

Fans passed through a lobby on their way into the arena. On each side were offices of Wake Forest coaches and athletic officials.

"When the games were there, they'd throw up a table and had that popcorn machine going full blast," Francis recalled.

"So many people who were there would talk about how the odor of the popcorn drifted through the gym."

Then there were nights when the smell of popcorn mingled with that of gunpowder.

"At one time when I was little, they signaled the end of the half and the end of the game by shooting off a starter's pistol borrowed from the track team," Greason, Jr. said. "And the smoke from that thing would then kind of permeate the atmosphere, and you would smell gunpowder for a minute or two."

Wake Forest's First Superstar

The biggest man on the Wake Forest campus in the 1930s stood 5-11, was president of the student body, married a professor's daughter and, because he had not received a scholarship, worked his way through school by waiting tables.

Incidentally, he also played forward for the Wake Forest basketball team, and played it well enough to lead the Southern Conference in scoring three straight years.

There was always more to Jim Waller than met the eye.

Harry Rabenhorst, an early football star and member of the Wake Forest Hall of Fame, was dispatched to Nashville, Tennessee in the mid-30s to watch Waller play high school basketball. Judging Waller to be too short for the college game, Rabenhorst recommended that Wake Forest not recruit him.

Undaunted, Waller enrolled at Wake Forest anyway and set about becoming the school's first real basketball superstar.

Though a half-foot shorter than many of his defenders, the left-handed Waller had an uncanny ability to get his trick hook shot off in traffic. Years later he explained his technique to a reporter for the *Winston-Salem Journal.*

"I'd set up three feet away, with the basket to my left," Waller said. "I'd get the ball, fake right, get the defensive man on my hip and then roll across the lane and hook."

His wife, Jan, said Waller was also an early master of working the officials.

"He had a way of moving his hips to foul people," she recalled. "Then he would hold up his hands to show he hadn't done anything."

Bones McKinney, later head coach at Wake Forest, confirmed Waller's ability to get the calls.

"Waller was the first man in this area to draw fouls with the pull-up shot," McKinney said, describing a two-handed underhand sweep. "He'd just bring his arms up until he hit the defensive man's arms."

Waller admitted his tactics were not always popular with opponents.

"The other teams' coaches always tried to get me called for charging," Waller said.

The Deacons, after struggling in the early 1930s, developed into a Southern Conference power once Waller arrived. They finished 15-6 in 1937, Waller's sophomore year, slumped to 7-12 in 1938, and then won the Southern Conference regular-season title with a 15-3 conference record in 1939.

Wake Forest, 18-6 overall, was upset by Clemson in the first round of the Southern Conference Tournament played at Raleigh Auditorium. The Deacons were unexpectedly invited anyway to play in the first NCAA Tournament, losing to Ohio State 64-52 in Waller's final game.

College basketball underwent radical rule changes during Waller's career, eliminating the center jump after each basket and changing from a leather basketball to one made of rubber. Waller said his game suffered with the change of equipment.

"The leather ball was deader," he said. "When you laid it up, it would roll around the rim and drop in. The new ball bounced off quicker."

Waller graduated from law school at Wake Forest and became police chief in Winston-Salem in 1950, six years before his alma mater relocated there. In 1962, after the Deacons beat Villanova in the regional final in College Park, Maryland, to reach the Final Four for the first time in history, a throng of fans met the team at Smith Reynolds Airport in Winston-Salem and caravanned back to campus.

Leading the escort was Jim Waller, the chief of police. Waller died in 1969 of cancer, at age 51.

The First Big Dance

There are ACC teams with better and more glorified records in NCAA Tournament play than Wake Forest.

The Deacons, however, can always say they were there first.

The season was 1939, a decade and a half before the inception of the ACC. It was many seasons before the term March Madness was coined, but by the second week of March in northern Wake County the Deacons were simply mad.

Seeded first in the Southern Conference Tournament with a 15-3 regular-season record, the Deacons were upended by Clemson 30-28 in the first round. Among the 3,941 on hand at Raleigh Auditorium for the upset was Ned Irish, who had arrived poised to invite the Deacons to a national tournament he had originated the season before called the National Invitational Tournament.

Having lost both the game and the invitation, Greason returned to Wake Forest and put the equipment and uniforms away. But the season received a commutation two days later, on Saturday, March 11, when Greason received a call from Coach Harold Olsen of Ohio State.

Olsen invited Greason and Wake Forest to compete in a tournament he was helping to organize called the NCAA Tournament. There was to be an eight-team field comprised of teams not invited to Irish's NIT.

Greason reassembled the team, the Deacons practiced on Monday and left via train Tuesday for Philadelphia and the

The 1939 team featured two firsts for the school: a basketball star in Jim Waller (No. 20), and a trip to the NCAA Tournament. (Courtesy of Wake Forest Media Relations)

Eastern Regional. The 12 players on board for the historic trip were captain Waller, Rex Carter, Smith Young, Vincent Convery, Stanley Apple, H.O. Barnes, Boyd Owen, Pete Nelson, Charles Yirinec, Bill Sweel, Dave Fuller and Pete Davis.

The opponent was Olsen's Ohio State Buckeyes, who had finished the regular season 14-6. The destination was Philadelphia's Palestra. The sendoff, according to Young, was provided by the entire 600-strong Wake Forest student body, one member of which had optimistically written "Wake Forest 100, Ohio State 50" on the side of the train.

In the first game of the regional semifinals, played in front of around 3,500 fans scattered throughout the 10,000-seat Palestra, Villanova beat Brown 42-30. The second game began well enough for the Deacons, who led 29-23 at halftime. Then Waller, the team's senior star and leading scorer, fouled out with seven minutes remaining and the Buckeyes rallied to a 64-52 victory.

Owen led Wake Forest with 19 points and Waller scored 14. The Deacons' nemesis that day was guard Dick Baker, who set a Palestra record with 25 points as the Buckeyes scored more than 50 points for only the fifth time of the season.

Baker, as it turned out, should have saved some energy for the national championship. After the Buckeyes beat Villanova 53-36 to advance to the title game against Oregon—played March 27 before around 5,000 spectators at Northwestern's Patton Gym in Evanston, Illinois—Baker was held scoreless as the Ducks rolled to a 46-33 victory and the first championship of the NCAA Tournament.

To have become such a national spectacle, the NCAA Tournament got off to an inauspicious start. During the game, Oregon's 5-8 guard Bobby Anet crashed into a courtside table and broke the tournament's championship trophy. When all the bills were paid the tournament lost $2,531, the one and only time the event ever failed to turn a profit.

"I'm Dickie Hemric"

Greason was such an avid hunter that as an assistant football coach on Jim Weaver's staff in the 1930s and 1940s, he would wear his hunting garb to practices.

When asked why, he responded, "So Weaver won't know which days I really go hunting."

As Wake Forest's basketball coach, Greason was known to combine his pursuits by hunting power forwards as well as deer and quail. On one excursion about two hours west of Wake Forest, he was riding through Yadkin County when he decided to check out a promising 6-6 high school senior from Jonesville named Dickie Hemric.

Greason pulled up to the Jonesville Grocery Store, where he asked the tall strapping young man behind the counter for directions to Jonesville High School.

"Why are you going there?" the young man asked.

"Because I want to see a basketball player named Dickie Hemric," Greason answered.

"Well you don't need directions," the young man said. "I'm Dickie Hemric."

Hemric did cast his lot with Wake Forest, but not before he tried out for a scholarship at N.C. State. Case, who built his legend on his keen eye for talent, proved on this occasion not to be as good a hunter as Greason.

Talk about one that got away. Hemric, by the time he graduated from Wake Forest in 1955, owned NCAA records for most career points (2,587), most career free-throw attempts (1,359), most career free throws made (905) and most free throws made in a season (302).

Better Than Anybody Could Have Dreamed

Like Tim Duncan around four decades later, Dickie Hemric flew to college basketball stardom under the radar of most recruiting experts. Because of Hemric's small-town background, and lack of imposing high school competition, there were those who wondered just how good he would be playing with the big boys of the Southern Conference.

Hemric, if the truth be told, also had his doubts. And because of them, he heavily considered attending Appalachian State.

"My first choice was Appalachian," Hemric said. "I had a lot of friends there, and I just felt the caliber of play in the old Southern Conference was a little beyond me. I was a junior before I played an appreciable amount of high school ball."

Once Hemric arrived on campus, planning to play both football and basketball, Greason was excited by what he saw. But Greason wasn't so excited that he immediately began touting Hemric for All-America honors. In Wake Forest's first two games of the 1951-52 season, against Hanes Hosiery and the Enka Rayonites, Hemric didn't start.

He broke into the lineup in the third game, at Tennessee, where the Deacons were pounded by the Volunteeers 77-53. But he handled himself well enough as a freshman to average 22.4 points and 18.6 rebounds and be named to All-Southern Conference first team.

Many have attributed Hemric's development as Wake Forest's first All-American to Greason's decision to hire McKinney as an assistant coach before the 1953 season. Greason had heard that McKinney, a former star at the University of North Carolina who played several seasons of professional basketball, was attending the Baptist Seminary on the Wake Forest campus.

McKinney, needing the $50 a week Wake Forest was paying for an assistant coach to help feed his four kids, accepted the position and went about teaching Hemric the finer points of post play.

"Dickie learned more in a month than any man I ever saw," McKinney said. "I don't know of any man who ever progressed as quickly as he did. When he came he did not have a hook and could not shoot a foul shot."

Taught by McKinney to shoot a hook with either hand, and pivot off either foot on inside moves to the basket, Hemric averaged 24.9 points as a sophomore, 24.3 as a junior and 27.6 as a senior.

And the better the competition, the better Hemric usually played. Three stars of the day were Cliff Hagan of Kentucky, Tom Gola of LaSalle and Jim Tucker of Duquesne.

In head-to-head matchups, Hemric outscored Hagan 28-18, Gola 23-20 and Tucker 23-15.

Dickie Hemric ended his Wake Forest career in 1955 with his name tattooed atop several NCAA scoring lists, including career points. (Courtesy of Wake Forest Media Relations)

The Ninth of 10 Kids

One of the most common feel-good stories of contemporary basketball is the kid from the bad streets who is able to escape the impoverishment of his upbringing because of his skills in the game. Often overlooked is the fact that players from earlier days in the game came from some rather humble backgrounds as well.

Hemric, Wake Forest's All-America center, was the ninth of 10 kids. His father was a carpenter in the rural town of Jonesville in Yadkin County. His five older brothers all joined the military. The newspaper routes he worked during his youth helped the family buy one pair of overalls for each Hemric child for school and one suit or dress for church.

When the knees of the overalls wore out, the pants were cut off for wear in the tobacco fields.

Working the Refs

The dressing room for officials at Gore Gym was downstairs beneath the playing court, just down the hall from the Wake Forest locker room. Rarely did referees work a game at Gore from 1952 through 1955 that they didn't get a pre-game visit from Hemric.

"I just want to welcome you gentlemen to the game tonight," Hemric would say, sticking his head in the door. "I'm just so glad you fellows are officiating this game. You're the best officials in the league."

Francis, the long-time publicist for Wake Forest and the ACC, laughed when remembering the story.

"Then he'd go back upstairs and ram everybody into the walls," Francis said. "And they wouldn't call any fouls on Dickie."

"It Was Very Much an Odd Couple"

If politics make for strange bedfellows, then so does basketball. The ACC has certainly never seen more of an odd couple than Wake Forest's head coach Greason and his assistant McKinney.

Greason was short, kindly and unassuming. McKinney was tall, colorful and loud. Yet, proving that opposites do indeed attract, the two made a wonderful team for the five years they coached together on the Wake Forest bench.

"It was very much an odd couple," said Maurice George, who played for Wake Forest from 1953 through 1955. "Coach Greason would just sit there and cross his legs and cross his arms and gripe every once in awhile.

"Bones did not take over the coaching. I never heard him say 'We have to do this.' He would always make a suggestion and Coach Greason had a choice of saying 'Yes,' or he could say 'No.' Bones did not overrule him."

They got together because their needs intersected. Greason, caught without an assistant, needed help coaching the Deacons. And McKinney, who at the time was a former NBA player with four kids attending the Southeastern Baptist Seminary on the Wake Forest campus, needed a job.

McKinney later recalled how he came to be hired in the spring of 1952.

"I had a newspaper route, the (Raleigh) *News and Observer*," McKinney recalled. "I wasn't making any money. People just didn't pay their bills. So I gave up that, because I couldn't stay awake in class.

"Dr. Bower had been his assistant, and he had gone to Indiana to get his doctor's degree. So (Greason) came up there.

"I said 'Oh, yes sir, Coach, I'd like to help you.'"

Greason told McKinney to report the next day to Athletics Director Weaver, who would fill him in on such little details as salary.

The Odd Couple: Coaches Greason, left, and McKinney. (Courtesy of Wake Forest Media Relations)

"I had started off in my mind, $4,000 to $4,500 or some-where around there," McKinney said. "I didn't know that was all Murray made. Finally I got it down to the realization that $750 would be $50 a week until the season was over.

"You know, I didn't tell anybody but the Lord. And that was exactly what Jim Weaver offered me, was $750. That's what I made the first year with Wake Forest. That got me through though."

Francis said that Greason had a particular duty in mind for McKinney. He wanted him to tutor a 6-6 freshman named Dickie Hemric on the finer aspects of play in the post.

"That's why Murray brought him in, for that purpose, to work with Hemric," Francis said. "I remember I went up to Gore gym and Bones was working with him. He was teaching him which way to move and all that. Bones was guarding him, and playing right with him."

As he related in his autobiography published in 1988 titled *Honk Your Horn If You Love Basketball*, mixing the two professions was not always easy.

"I coached during the week and at the games on Saturday night," McKinney wrote. "Then I got up the next morning, drove 50 miles to a little Baptist church and preached a good old 'knock-down' Baptist sermon. I learned the sermon while driving my 1947 Ford 80 miles an hour to the church.

"I held a cigarette in one hand and a Pepsi in the other. My sermon notes were taped to the dashboard. I don't know who was driving. It must have been the Lord because I sure wasn't. I apologize to all those people I ran off the road in those days, but now they know why."

Granny's Got Game

McKinney was a junior center for North Carolina in 1946, the year the Tar Heels reached the championship game of the NCAA Tournament. Standing in their way was Oklahoma A&M and its 6-10 All-America center Bob Kurland.

As the Tar Heels got ready to take the court in Madison Square Garden, assistant coach Pete Mullis reviewed the defensive assignments.

"And you McKinney, get on that Kurland," Mullis instructed. "That seven-foot clown is so bad that he couldn't even score a basket against his grandmother."

Try as he might, McKinney couldn't keep Kurland from scoring 23 points. And trying as hard as he did, McKinney fouled out after scoring only five points himself.

In the somber locker room following the Tar Heels' 43-40 defeat, McKinney couldn't help laughing at his coach, his performance and ultimately, himself.

"I was just thinking of something, Pete," he said, spotting Mullis across the room. "That guy's grandma must be a whale of a basketball player."

"A Great Night in Old Gore"

A half-century later, Murray Greason, Jr., still remembered the clammy, wet uniform under his clothes and how it chilled his teenage body as he raced across the North Carolina countryside to see his father's team play basketball.

Wake Forest High School had just finished a game and Murray, Jr., who played on the team, was in a great rush. It was December 9, 1952, and the legendary Case had brought his N.C. State Wolfpack to town to play Wake Forest College.

"We got through with our game, and I just threw my jeans on over my shorts," Murray, Jr. recalled. "I didn't take off anything. I ran across country and got in that side door just as they blew the game over."

The game he just missed was a classic. The Deacons, led by sophomores Hemric and Jack Williams, beat Case's Wolfpack 51-50, and the cozy confines of Gore Gymnasium were still buzzing with the electricity of the grand victory.

"And then it became apparent that something else was about to happen, because most of the crowd did not leave," Murray, Jr. said.

His father, the man whose name he shared, was three games into his 20th season as Wake Forest's head basketball coach. Supporters of the program had decided to honor Murray, Sr., for his service to his alma mater.

As his son watched from the dense, expectant crowd, Greason was hoisted by two football players, Joe Koch and Bob Gaona and carried through the crowd to center court. There he was presented with a television set, a deep fat cooker and an 11-foot refrigerator stocked with frozen food.

Outside, in the parking lot, the moonlight reflected off the chrome of a 1952 Ford stationwagon.

"Of course that made my family very happy," Murray, Jr. said. "Because on that six or seven thousand dollars a year (salary) we couldn't afford the television or the car.

"So that was a great night in Old Gore."

Winning a Championship To Go

As well as the 1952-53 season began, with fans and supporters showering Greason with gifts following a victory over N.C. State, it ended even better. In the last Southern Conference game played before Wake Forest and seven other schools broke off to form the Atlantic Coast Conference, the Deacons beat N.C. State 71-70 for the conference championship.

The Deacons, led by sophomores Hemric and Williams, stomped North Carolina 89-63 on February 17 and finished the regular season 18-6 overall and seeded second in the Southern Conference Tournament with a 12-3 league mark. They beat Richmond 85-70 in the quarterfinals and Maryland 61-59 in the semifinals to earn a date with the 13th-ranked Wolfpack in the title game.

College basketball, from 1952 through 1954, was played in quarters. Wake Forest led 36-34 at halftime, and 56-54 after three quarters. The Wolfpack, springing a full-court press, rallied to outscore the Deacons 11-4 for a 65-60 lead. Greason's counter strategy was to shelve his zone defense for an aggressive man to man, and Wake Forest responded with eight straight points for a 68-65 lead.

The tension was all but unbearable when N.C. State, trailing 71-70, fouled Wake Forest's Jim DeVos with 10 seconds remaining. DeVos, a reserve, missed both free throws to give the Wolfpack a chance. The victory was saved, however, when an alert Williams stole an N.C. State pass. With the victory, Greason became the only Southern Conference coach to beat Case twice in the same season.

"This beats the thrill of catching an eight-pound bass," Greason said afterward. "It's the best thing that's ever happened to me in basketball, and I've been coaching at Wake Forest 20 years."

Chapter 2
The Early
ACC Years

Twelve Letters

Before he became head basketball coach at Wake Forest, resurrecting the program to its early glory, Murray Greason was one of the school's most celebrated athletes. From 1921, when he showed up as an undergraduate, to 1926 when he graduated from Wake Forest law school, Greason won 12 varsity letters in football, basketball and baseball.

He was team captain in football and basketball.

Though he didn't play football at Wake Forest High School because the school wasn't big enough to field a team, Greason soon became a star halfback in college. His greatest claim to fame was a 72-yard touchdown run off tackle that beat North Carolina 7-6 in 1924 for the Baptists' first victory over their rivals from Chapel Hill in more than 30 years.

That same season, he broke his nose in a game at Washington and Lee and still played the entire 60 minutes.

In early 2004, Greason's son, Murray Greason, Jr., was looking through a drawer for tax receipts when he came across a commemoration to his father's athletic prowess.

"I opened a little box I had there that I hadn't opened in years," said Murray, Jr. "I had forgotten I had this thing. And it's a little football made to be worn on your keychain. It's gold with a big black W. Engraved around the rest of the football it said 'Greason, 1924 All-State halfback.'

"For a no-publicity school like Wake Forest with Red Grange running around up in Chicago, that wasn't bad."

Eschewing the law, Greason, upon completion of school, played professional baseball. Jack Horner of the *Durham Herald*, writing in 1960, remembered Greason as his childhood hero.

"I first knew Murray Greason as a kid batboy for the Fayetteville Highlanders and he was the team's star second baseman, fresh off the Wake Forest campus during the summer of 1926," Horner wrote. "Greason was a slick fielder, sharp hitter and fiery competitor.

"While he was my hero back then, I later had the pleasure and privilege of covering many of his team's performances and observing his kindly and fatherly handling of some of Wake Forest's greatest athletes. In victory and defeat, I admired his gentlemanly coaching habits. He was a man of great character."

By that fall, Greason had taken a job coaching basketball at Lexington, N.C., where he met Elizabeth Hackney, best known as Lib. The two were married on August 15, 1932.

"He met my mother while she was a high school student, but he didn't marry her until she had gone off to WC (Women's College) for a couple of years," Murray, Jr. recalled.

Greason returned to Wake Forest in 1934 to be the head basketball coach and assistant football coach. He remained on the football staff as the backfield coach until 1948, and somehow found time to also coach baseball from 1940 to 1947.

Rock Brinkley, a one-time Wake Forest athlete who later became head of the Deacon Club, said Greason was a hard person to dislike, but an easy person to love.

"He was about as nice a fellow as I've ever been connected with at Wake Forest," Brinkley said. "In all the troubles we had over there, he was one fellow that nobody had anything but good words for.

"He meant a great deal to me both on and off the field."

The Duncan of His Day

So just how good was Dickie Hemric?

Decades after he scored his last of 2,587 points for Wake Forest, and grabbed his last of 1,802 rebounds, there's a tendency to view Hemric's accomplishments with the same discernment, if not skepticism, one might employ to assess Jack Chesbro's 41 victories for the 1904 New York Highlanders. Hemric, like Chesbro, performed in an era much different from today, under rules conducive to his particular abilities.

The free throw lane during Hemric's career was but six-feet wide, half the width found on today's standard court. That allowed the bullish 6-6, 227-pound Hemric to operate more freely closer to the basket.

And during Hemric's senior season of 1955, an experimental rule allotted the offensive team an inside position along the lane on free throws. Players were known to miss free throws on the side of the basket closest to their teammate, thus padding both the rebound and point totals.

That said, there were 14 ACC players in 1955 at least as tall as Hemric, and eight players even taller. And none of them averaged 27.6 points and 19.0 rebounds, Hemric's statistics for the season.

And few, if any, showed the heart of Hemric, who played his entire career on a Gore Gymnasium court built on a shin-rattling cement base. In one of the most courageous performances in ACC history, Hemric scored 44 points against Duke in 1954 on what was later diagnosed as a broken ankle.

Another time, a stray elbow from N.C. State's 6-10 Cliff Dwyer cost Hemric a couple of teeth.

Tiring finally of the terrific physical abuse he was taking, Hemric retaliated one night at Virginia by whacking a Cavalier across the nose with his elbow. The referees didn't see the infraction, but the fans who did bombarded the court with cups of ice.

Whatever historians think of Hemric, those who played with or against him certainly recognized his abilities. He was Player of the Year in each of the first two years of the ACC, he was the first player to have his jersey (No. 24) retired by Wake Forest, and he was the first Deacon to be drafted by the NBA.

Coach Frank McGuire of North Carolina said that to ask a Tar Heel to shut Hemric down was to assign an impossible task.

"That guy is going to score about 30 or more points against you, regardless, so why bother to concentrate on him?" McGuire reasoned. "We just try to stop other guys on the team."

In the late 1980s, officials at Wake Forest mounted what, sadly, proved to be an unsuccessful campaign to have Hemric enshrined in the Naismith Basketball Hall of Fame in Springfield, Massachusetts. Sports information director John Justus asked venerable sportswriter Dick Herbert to write a letter of recommendation to Joe O'Brien, the executive director of the Hall of Fame.

Herbert responded with the following testimonial:

"Dear Mr. O'Brien,

"It has come to my attention that Dick Hemric of Wake Forest has been nominated for the Hall of Fame.

"I support the nomination enthusiastically.

"I was sports editor of the *Raleigh News and Observer* for 29 years (1942-71) and covered all the great players in the area. I know of no player in the Atlantic Coast Conference who had a greater impact on his team and college basketball than Hemric. You have the record of his accomplishments and I do not need to go into them.

"In addition to his basketball ability, he was one of the nicest athletes I have ever known. He was very successful in business. He is a true credit to basketball and deserves its highest honor.

"Cordially,

"Dick Herbert."

The ACC's First Famous Lefty

Mention the name Lefty, and most ACC basketball fans automatically think of Lefty Driesell, the head coach at Maryland from 1970 through 1986.

But it wasn't always that way.

The first famous Lefty in the league was Lowell "Lefty" Davis of Wake Forest, one of the most versatile athletes in the early years of the conference.

A 6-2 forward who averaged 18.6 points and 7.2 rebounds from 1954 through 1956, Davis also pitched for the Wake Forest baseball team and competed for the Deacons' track team. He was good enough on the mound to win 10 games and lose only one during the 1955 season.

But because Davis had skipped too many mandatory chapel services, he was not allowed to fly to Omaha for the 1955 College World Series. A compromise was struck between the administration and athletics department where Davis was allowed to pitch for the Deacons in weekend games as long as he was back in class by Monday morning.

Davis shut out Colorado State 10-0, and returned east to listen on the radio as the Deacons won three of their next four to capture the 1955 national title.

A basketball teammate, Jackie Murdock, remembers two of Davis's most pronounced qualities, his versatility and his toughness.

"When the school was in old Wake Forest, he went to a track meet at State to pole vault and high jump in the morning," Murdock said. "In the afternoon, he went back to Wake Forest and pitched three innings against State in baseball. We won the game."

In the rough and tumble of college basketball, Davis more than held his own. Despite weighing only 153 pounds, he averaged at least seven rebounds a game as a sophomore, junior and senior.

"I remember one basketball game against Duke when he was going in for a layup, got hit and broke his nose," Murdock said. "They took him downstairs, and got him straightened out. He came back up with his eyes full of tears from the blow he took, but he hit three straight jumpers."

Davis, who hailed from Johnston City, Illinois, returned to his home state to work as a drafting supervisor for AT&T Information Systems in Naperville. He was killed in an automobile accident in Oklahoma City in 1986, 11 years after being inducted in the Wake Forest Hall of Fame.

E Means Empty

The usual mode of transportation for college basketball teams, for years, was the automobile. Three lanky players would crawl into the front of one of the touring sedans of the time, and three would crawl into the back, and off they'd head for the next game.

Wake Forest played at Virginia one evening, and was returning from Charlottesville to Winston-Salem. Greason drove the first leg of the trip, but after tiring, turned the wheel over to one of his players, Henry Bowers.

Greason, having slid over to the middle of the front seat, promptly fell asleep.

The car was approaching Danville, Virginia just north of the state line when the engine started sputtering and finally stalled out. As Bowers was pulling over, Greason woke up.

"What's wrong?" Greason asked.

"Coach, we ran out of gas," Bowers replied.

"Well Henry, didn't you watch the gauge?" Greason asked him.

"Yeah Coach," Bowers answered. "But I didn't want to wake you up."

Louder Asleep Than Awake

A quiet man by nature, Greason was known for making more noise asleep than awake.

"When he went to sleep he snored," long-time Wake Forest publicist Marvin "Skeeter" Francis remembered. "And he really, really snored."

A common courtesy teams used to provide for opponents was what was known as "local hospitality," which consisted of a room or two of bunks where the visitors could rest up during the afternoon for a night game. The team would file in, get a rolled up mattress, sheets, pillow and pillow case and find somewhere to sack out.

The more experienced Deacons knew that, if they wanted any rest, they needed to stake out an area as far away from their coach as possible.

"So we had a guy named Jo Ladd," Francis recalled. "And I remember that somebody said, 'Jo, you'd better not get too close down there or Coach Murray will snore you out of the bed.' And Jo said, 'Oh, it's not going to bother me. My dad was a great snorer and I always got to sleep.'

"About that time Murray turned over and started snoring. A little while later we looked up and here comes Jo down the aisle with his sheets. He said he couldn't stand it."

Bones McKinney, an assistant coach in the mid-1950s, said that if the team were allotted two rooms, then Greason would often awake to find himself in a room by himself.

"Oh man, he could suck up a mattress cover," McKinney said. "It was just unbelievable what that man could do.

"I don't know how Lib, his wife, ever went to sleep."

High on the Hog

The athletics budgets of college programs are so big today that most have to have a little pork in them somewhere. McKinney used to tell the story of how Greason tried to keep the pork out of his program.

"I went with him one time to raise money for the Deacon Club," McKinney said. "When we got down to eastern North Carolina, the guy knew what he was coming for.

"He said 'Well, Murray, what do you want this time? Do you want money or do you want a hog?'

"Murray said, 'I reckon you'd better give me the hog. I'd have to turn the money in.'"

Murray's Precious Pack

Losses dogged Greason more than he would ever let on. Though outwardly placid and empathetic, even in the most tumultuous of times, Greason would become so wrought up before a game that he couldn't eat.

"Murray sits at the supper table and often he doesn't touch a thing," his wife, Lib, once said. "He just sits there quietly, or he may become a little nauseated. No matter what I prepare, it's always the same with Murray."

What never dogged Greason, however, were his dogs, his collection of beagles that was always fed at the Greason household before the human residents sat down to the table. Francis said he could remember Greason sitting on the steps of Gore

Gymnasium at the old campus, blissfully asleep surrounded by his precious pack.

Frank Spencer, the sports editor of the *Winston-Salem Journal*, said Greason once promised him a pup from a new litter. Greason's wife, Lib, heard the promise and scoffed.

"Don't count on that," she told Spencer. "He never let a dog get away from him that he ever had."

Many years later, a smile creased the face of Greason, Jr., when he heard the story. A graduate of Wake Forest, Greason, Jr. played on the Deacons' freshman team and was also a student manager for McKinney.

"He would give away things like our furniture, but not his dogs," Greason, Jr. said. "One player got married between years and the wife, who was also a student, her family didn't like it so much. So they were really scraping by.

"My father gave them our kitchen table because they didn't have one. I mean, we had a way to get another one.

"That was the kind of guy he was."

Scratching Backs

Wake Forest drove to Richmond one day for a game against the University of Richmond, and the players were eating lunch at the hotel when one of the them noticed a car getting towed.

"Coach," he said to Greason, "isn't that your car?"

"Yeah, I'll be doggone, I believe it is," Greason replied.

Greason, after finishing the eggs on the plate in front of him, went with other members of the traveling party to retrieve his car. They found a policeman on the streets of Richmond, who directed them to the lot where the car had been towed.

A cab was hailed to carry them to the lot, where they confronted another policeman assigned to guard the gate.

By way of explanation, Greason mentioned he was the head basketball coach at Wake Forest, and that his Deacons needed to get their car out to make it to the game against Richmond.

The policeman said: "I was thinking about going out to that game tonight to see you folks play."

Greason answered: "You were? There will be two tickets for you at the gate when you get there."

The policeman said: "That's very nice of you, Coach."

Greason said: "So how much do we owe you to get the car out?"

The policeman responded: "Not a thing. Not a thing."

Cooling His Heels in Fairbanks

Few, if any, basketball players at Wake Forest have seen their careers take a more dramatic detour than Jack Williams.

Williams's detour actually took him through a two-year service stint in Alaska.

After averaging 20.2 points and 8.1 rebounds as a sophomore in 1953, to help lead the Deacons to the Southern Conference championship, Williams, a 6-3 forward, was considered one of the top players in the fledging Atlantic Coast Conference going into his junior season. But his junior season, as it turned out, would have to wait for two years.

Enrolled in ROTC to secure his college deferment, Williams failed to appear for exercises scheduled for the lawn of Hunter Dorm on the old campus in the spring of 1953. Williams later told friends that he missed the pushups and jumping jacks because he was playing marbles.

When questioned by the ROTC colonel, Williams explained that he was simply "cutting class." The colonel responded by revoking Williams's deferment and Greason, try as he might, could not get it restored.

Inducted immediately after the semester, Williams was stationed in Fairbanks, Alaska. While cooling his heels in America's last frontier, Williams managed to keep his skills somewhat sharp by playing on a Pan-American team.

He returned in time for the 1956 season, and averaged 16.5 points as a junior and 16.2 as a senior.

"When he came back he was about a step slower," said Greason, Jr. "It was just high living or something, I guess. But in 1953 he was as good as anybody I had ever seen. He wasn't all that big, but he could jump.

"And he could move to the hole in a whole lot of different ways."

The Deacons of 1954 survived Williams's absence as junior Hemric averaged 24.3 points and 15.1 rebounds and sophomore Davis averaged 17.4 points and 7.2 rebounds. Playing a brutal schedule, they finished the regular season with a 15-11 overall mark and 8-4 record in ACC play.

Seeded third, the Deacons stirred the pot in the first ACC Tournament by playing three overtime games. After beating South Carolina 58-57 in the quarterfinals, and Maryland 64-56 in the semifinals, they rallied from a 16-point deficit in the championship against Everett Case's N.C. State Wolfpack, and had three shots to win at the end of regulation.

All three shots missed their mark, and Wake Forest lost the league's first title game 82-80.

"I'm Not Going to Let Him Up"

It may well have been his intention, but Coach McGuire of North Carolina had his own special ability of rubbing others the wrong way. Playing against the cocky, self-assured New Yorker with the thick Yankee accent and high-dollar suits was so exasperating, that even a coach with such a well-mannered disposition as Greason could learn things about himself he might not want to know.

Greason's Deacons were playing McGuire's Tar Heels in the semifinals of the 1956 ACC Tournament in Raleigh's Reynolds Coliseum. Wake Forest, riding the wave of 10 victories in its previous 12 games, was playing its best basketball of a really good season. The Deacons, led by Davis, Williams, Murdock, Ernie Wiggins and Jim Gilley finished ranked No. 16 in the nation with a 19-9 record.

Greason's son, Murray Jr., recalled a conversation between his father and assistant coach McKinney as the Deacons stormed to an intensely gratifying 77-56 victory.

"Carolina had beaten us the year before, and Frank McGuire had been quoted as saying some things that didn't sit well over on the Wake Forest side," Murray Jr. said. "And my father was relatively mild mannered.

"With three or four minutes to go we're beating them by 20-something points and Bones leans over and says, 'Coach, we've got them. Why don't you send some of these boys down on the end of the bench in there and let them play a little bit?'

"My father said, 'Nope. I've got the son of a bitch right where I want him, and I'm not going to let him up.'"

Bones Pulls a Fast One—On Himself

As quick as McKinney was to tell stories on other people, he was even quicker to tell them on himself.

An avid golfer, McKinney was playing in a tournament once in Durham and was tied with his opponent on the 18th tee.

"He hit a drive into the woods and I began to smile," McKinney recalled.

McKinney helped look for his ball for about 20 minutes until suddenly the guy yelled 'Here it is,' chipped onto the green and dropped the putt to beat McKinney by one stroke.

"You know something," McKinney later recounted. "That guy cheated. But I couldn't say anything because I had his ball in my pocket two minutes after we started looking for it."

Relocating a College

A question often asked by basketball fans across the country is "Where exactly is Wake Forest?"

The answer? Not in Wake Forest.

But it used to be.

After educating students for 112 years on a campus located in Wake County, some 15 miles from Raleigh, the school up and moved to Winston-Salem in the summer of 1956. The unusual migration culminated a 10-year plan that began in March of 1946 when the Z. Smith Reynolds Foundation offered upwards of $350,000 annually—pretty serious pocket change in those days—to entice the college to build a campus and relocate to Winston-Salem, 110 miles to the west.

By the end of the year, the board of trustees and the Baptist State Convention approved, and began raising money for the move. Ground was broken at the new campus on October 15, 1951, on an allotted portion of the estate of Richard Joshua and Katherine Reynolds. On hand for the ceremony was President Harry Truman, who dug the first shovelful of dirt. Also present was President Dr. Harold Tribble of Wake Forest, whose advocacy of the move had drawn the ire of those people at the college who liked things exactly the way they had been.

"The general sentiment was we didn't want to move," recalls Greason Jr., who was born and raised in Wake Forest. "We were happy and comfortable.

"As one man put it, 'I didn't want to come because people up here didn't know how to do barbeque, and I found out pretty quickly that the soil was red mud. It's hard to work in it.'

"Harold Tribble had to come across basically as heartless because it was his job."

In time, Greason said, he came to realize the wisdom in Tribble's decision. A half-century later, Wake Forest College, now named Wake Forest University, is a thriving private institution of around 4,000 undergraduates playing competitive basketball in college basketball's most competitive conference.

"It was just a sentiment of a loss," said Abe Elmore, a student in the early '50s who served as equipment manager for the football and basketball teams. "But I think now that we're getting older, we've about gotten over it."

A Sneak Peek at the Future

A caravan of 11 buses carrying 400 students departed the old Wake Forest campus at 4 p.m. on December 6, 1955.

Its destination was the future.

The trip required three hours.

Although the college would not officially relocate from Wake County to Winston-Salem until six months later, the intrepid 400 wanted to get a sneak peek at the new arena, called Memorial Coliseum, that had already been built only a mile or so from the new campus. The occasion was Wake Forest's home basketball game against N.C. State.

The students were leaving a tumultuous campus behind. Pat Preston, the director of athletics, had just resigned amid media reports that Wake Forest planned to de-emphasize athletics. Also, the school had decided not to renew the contract of football coach Tom Rogers, who had just completed a 5-4-1 season.

Tempers ran so hot that students burned an effigy of Tribble, the school's president, while Tribble watched.

Upon arrival in Winston-Salem, the students were fired up for a game between the Deacon team that had lost its opener to

George Washington and a Wolfpack squad that was ranked third following victories over Florida State and Penn State.

The first game of Memorial Coliseum was actually played between the freshmen teams, with the Wolfpack Cubs beating the Baby Deacs 72-60.

The starting lineup for Wake Forest varsity was Wiggins, Murdock, Gilley, Davis and Jack Williams, just back from his two-year stint in the service. Coach Everett Case of N.C. State started Ronnie Shavlik, Vic Molodet, John Maglio, Phil DiNardo and Cliff Hafer.

The Wolfpack, which would finish 24-4 that season and win its third straight ACC title, defeated Wake Forest 90-81. The visitors were apparently undaunted by a fan, William Shepherd of Winston-Salem, who was seen walking around with a Wolf's head in a noose.

Afterward Case was asked what he thought of Wake Forest's home to be.

"Just fine," Case responded. "The lights on the basketball court could be a little better, and my feet are a little damp from wading through that water just outside our dressing room, but I'm not complaining or criticizing anything. Those are just some of the bugs that pop up when you open a new building like this.

"Oh, we had plenty of things wrong with our coliseum in Raleigh when we opened it, but everything worked out in time."

The White Elephant

When Wake Forest moved to Winston-Salem before the 1956-57 season, the Deacons needed a place to play basketball. An organization called the Winston-Salem Foundation was charged with building one.

Unfortunately the facility, known as Memorial Coliseum, was built for a song. And the title of that song, sung most memorably by Peggy Lee, was "Is That All There Is?"

The original estimate for the arena was $500,000. Duke, a decade and a half earlier, had built what is today known as Cameron Indoor Stadium for $400,000.

But building costs soared in the postwar boom of the 1950s, and the Winston-Salem Foundation found that not even the $1.25 million it raised in donations would cover all the costs. So it struck from the blueprint plans to build a bay in the front of the building and two balconies.

Strapped for cash, the Foundation cut a deal with Wake Forest where the school would provide operating costs for Memorial Coliseum in exchange for using the arena as many as 30 dates a year at costs.

The deal expired by the early 1960s, and by 1968 the Foundation was desperate to unload what one member called "The White Elephant." It paid the city of Winston-Salem $75,000 to take over the operations of the Coliseum and adjacent fairgrounds.

Never considered the Taj Mahal of basketball, Memorial Coliseum really began to show its age after ice was added beneath the hardwood in the early 1970s to accommodate a series of minor-league hockey teams. Dank and dark, the arena smelled like an overflowing clothes hamper.

"I think if they hadn't put ice in it, it would have been able to remain pretty acceptable for a while," said Gene Hooks, the director of athletics at Wake Forest from 1964 until 1992. "The fact it had ice, and didn't have a budget to maintain it, made it hard to deal with from the standpoint of mildew, decay and just the way the place smelled."

By the 1980s, Memorial Coliseum had become such a liability to the program that Wake Forest began playing selected home games at Greensboro Coliseum, 25 miles to the east. The Deacons played 51 "home games" in Greensboro from 1982 until Joel Coliseum was opened before the 1989-90 season.

The 8,200-seat Memorial Coliseum, which could be hot and cacophonous on its best nights, was actually not an easy place for opponents to play. The Deacons won 250 games there and lost 94 for a winning percentage of .727.

Still there were few tears shed when the White Elephant was finally torn down to make more room for the Joel Coliseum parking lot.

"I have a hard time being nostalgic about that building," Hooks said.

Going Way Back

If Murdock was born to play basketball, then he was bred really early to play the sport for McKinney.

It's hard to imagine a stronger mentor/protégé relationship than that of McKinney and Murdock. The two first met when Murdock was 11, and McKinney was the coach of his youth baseball team in Raleigh.

Murdock, only 5-10, 152 pounds during his playing days at Wake Forest, was so small at 11 years old that McKinney feigned concern that he might get lost in the outfield weeds. But Murdock could tell right off he was playing for a big man.

Murdock, though a Duke fan at the time, was quickly taken by McKinney, then a pro basketball player in the NBA.

"He was tough and worked us hard, but we won the championship," Murdock recalled. "We kept up with each other off and on after that.

"When I got ready to go to college he came over to see me and talked about going to Wake Forest. He was helping Coach Greason at the time. I felt I would have a better chance to play at Wake Forest so I went there."

A natural athlete who excelled at every sport he pursued, Murdock was the Deacons' floor leader during his three seasons of varsity eligibility. In 1956, as a junior, he led the ACC in both field-goal accuracy (50 percent) and free-throw accuracy (85.7 percent). The feat wasn't accomplished again in the league until

Greg Manning of Maryland shot 64.3 percent from the floor and 90.8 percent from the line in 1980.

Murdock was second-team All-ACC as a junior and first-team as a senior, the season he also was named All-America.

"He was a competitor before he could spell the word," McKinney said of Murdock.

Murdock returned to serve as an assistant coach under McKinney from 1961 through 1965. When McKinney left before the 1966 season, he was succeeded by his protégé, who coached the Deacons for one season.

Murdock was inducted in the Wake Forest Hall of Fame in 1982 and into the North Carolina Hall of Fame in 1990.

"You Could Hear the Flesh Cracking"

Anybody who described basketball as a non-contact sport certainly wasn't watching the game as it was played in the ACC during the 1950s and 1960s. Fights and downright brawls were so common that the term "shots taken" described fist blows to the head as accurately as field-goal or free-throw attempts. Often fans either instigated or inflamed the violence as the still-fledging ACC struggled with security issues in small, hot and at times, far too intimate gymnasiums.

North Carolina proved to be a particularly hostile place for the Deacons to play, as anyone who attended Wake Forest's game in Chapel Hill on February 15, 1956 could attest. The game, which the 10th-ranked Tar Heels won 77-73, was winding down when Wake Forest's Bill Tucker and North Carolina's Bob Cunningham became entangled, in the vernacular of the times, near mid-court.

Suddenly fans in North Carolina's Woollen Gym swarmed out of the stands and fights broke out everywhere. One eyewitness recounted, "All at once spectators come sailing out of the stands like a bunch of chickens and went round and round on the court."

McKinney, still a Deacons' assistant to head coach Murray Greason, watched in awe.

"Man, there were fists flying everywhere," McKinney remarked. "You could hear the flesh cracking. It was difficult to distinguish pugilists from would-be peacemakers."

The hospitality was so lacking that Coach McGuire of North Carolina felt compelled to make his way to the visiting locker room and apologize to the visitors. McGuire told the media the fracas overwhelmed all his attempts to control it.

"I didn't know who was fighting who—and I don't believe anybody else knew either," McGuire said. "All I know is that I got hit in the head a couple of times and got a kick on my leg a few times. I couldn't stop the fight."

ACC Commissioner Jim Weaver reviewed film of the donnybrook and suspended Tucker and Cunningham for the remainder of the season. He also fined each school $500 and reprimanded them for "unsportsmanlike conduct."

The road trip to Duke that season also turned out to be eventful when fans showered the court with apple cores and coins. Duke's Ronnie Mayer and official Cart Howerton were struck by apple cores, but the real victim was Wake Forest's Gilley, who slipped on an apple core and pulled a leg muscle.

Not a Dry Eye in the Room

North Carolina's perfect 32-0 National Championship season of 1957 was an example of how perfection, like beauty, often rests in the eye of the beholder.

For in the tear-stained eyes of the Wake Forest players following the semifinals of the ACC Tournament, the only thing perfect about North Carolina's unforgettable 61-59 victory over the Deacons in Reynolds Coliseum was a perfectly unforgivable crime perpetrated by official Jim Mills.

Passions, as usual, were running high when the Deacons and Tar Heels met for the fourth time of the season. North Carolina had won the previous three, prevailing 63-55 on December 29 in the Dixie Classic, 72-69 on February 13 in Chapel Hill and 69-64 on February 26 in Winston-Salem.

Author Ron Morris revealed in *ACC Basketball: An Illustrated History* how instead of invoking the three victories, McGuire chose to motivate his No. 1-ranked Tar Heels by recalling their 77-56 drubbing by the Deacons in the semifinals of the 1956 Tournament.

"Wake Forest is a big opponent of mine," McGuire railed to his troops. "I have not forgotten how those boys celebrated last year in this building, how they humiliated us. We've had such a great, great year. Don't let them spoil the year for you.

"They'll do anything, anything to try and win. We've never had an easy game against Wake, those sons of bitches. I've never had an easy game against Wake Forest. It's a big thing for them to beat us. They play like they're possessed."

And by doing so once again, Wake Forest possessed a 59-58 lead with 55 seconds remaining after Gilley, a 6-6 senior from Winston-Salem, made both ends of a one and one. The Deacons had trailed 22-11 early, they'd been out-rebounded an unfathomable 29-8 in the first half, and they had survived a wild second-half despite not getting even one field goal after halftime from their senior leader Murdock.

Now, by outscoring the Tar Heels 6-0 over 82 frantic seconds, they stood less than a minute from ending North Carolina's season.

North Carolina inbounded the ball after Gilley's second free throw and attacked the basket. McGuire chose not to call time as he watched guard Tommy Kearns dribble upcourt. Len Rosenbluth received a pass left of the lane, planted his left foot just inside the lane and arched a hook shot toward the basket. A millisecond later, he collided with Wendell Carr, a reserve forward from Muncie, Indiana, who was in the game because starter Williams had fouled out. As the ball swished through the net, the crowd roared so loudly as to drown out the officials' whistles.

Gilley and Broadway stared at Mills, the official closest to the play. Mills walked to the scorers' table and made his call: Blocking on Carr.

What followed was an uproar that, in some circles, will never subside.

Rosenbluth, awarded the basket, made the free throw for a 61-59 lead with 46 seconds left. If the call had gone against Rosenbluth, Carr would have been awarded free throws under rules of the day that did not take into account offensive possession.

With time running down, Wiggins missed a 20-footer. The rebound came off the rim and the ball got knocked around. Finally Bob Cunningham of North Carolina gained control of the prize and dribbled to midcourt as time expired.

McKinney hid his face in his hands as he exited the court. The sportswriters who entered the Wake Forest locker room found a room full of Deacons with their reddened eyes staring at their feet.

Davis, a Deacon forward who had graduated the year before, entered the room and all but ran the media out.

"Can't you see these fellows are eating their hearts out?" Davis demanded. "Why don't you get out and leave them alone? The real story, as you surely must know, is the way the referees choked up."

Bill Gibson, Wake Forest's director of athletics, requested that everyone but those on the team leave, and McKinney made his way around the room hugging every player.

Thirty years later, McKinney could still feel the pain in the room.

"That place was like a tomb," he recalled. "Of all my days in the pros, all my playing and all my coaching days, this was the saddest moment of my entire basketball career. The whole damn place was broken up. I've never seen anything like it in my life. There wasn't one dry eye in the place, mine included.

"To be honest, I've always thought God had a hand in that game. I don't think He cares a whole lot about ACC basketball, but I think He had something to do with that one."

So did Mills make the right call? Apparently even he wasn't sure.

"At the time, I didn't think I missed the call," Mills said. "But I've heard so much about it since. I wonder now. Maybe I missed it because Bones has always wanted me to look at the film."

To McKinney, there was no doubt.

"I'll always contend Rosenbluth drove into Carr," McKinney said. "The film clearly showed it. There's no question about it."

Rosenbluth, when asked, was diplomatic.

"It was a very, very close play," Rosenbluth said. "It would have been a shame if we had lost the whole year on a charging foul. That would have been a shame. But the way we won games, we probably would have intercepted a pass and won the game, anyway."

McGuire, for his part, was just glad the call went his team's way. After his Tar Heels beat Final Four opponents Michigan State and Kansas—both in three overtimes—to win the national championship, McGuire made no bones about how hard it was to beat Murray Greason and the Demon Deacons.

Talking to a television reporter after the championship, McGuire called Wake Forest the toughest team the Tar Heels had played all season.

The Means to be Mean

College basketball, as it was played in the late 1950s and early 1960s, could be a mean game. To play it well, a team often had to have the means to be mean.

And from the time he showed up as a freshman in the fall of 1956 until he graduated in the spring of 1960, Dave Budd provided Wake Forest those means.

"He took no shit from anybody," teammate Billy Packer recalled. "But he wasn't a hachet man at all.

"He was a good player."

Budd played for weak teams as a sophomore and junior, but was still around as a senior in 1960 when the influx of two talented sophomores, Packer and center Len Chappell, helped transform the Deacons back into an ACC power. He averaged 13.5 points and 9.1 rebounds in 75 varsity games, and was second-team All-ACC as a sophomore and senior.

"He was a hell of an athlete, a great athlete," Packer said. "He was a great leaper, good hands. He was very strong, 6-7, 220 pounds."

But whether he was anxious, or just willing, to mix it up, Budd figured prominently in the more memorable fights that broke out during games of that era. After his notable participation in a brawl against North Carolina in Winston-Salem in 1959, Budd was placed on probation by the ACC. Commissioner Weaver ruled one more transgression and Budd would be banished for good.

"His senior year he had to play with kid gloves all the time, because he was under the threat of suspension," Packer said.

But coaches and teammates alike insisted that Budd was a helluva guy, who just happened to be a victim of circumstances. McKinney felt so strongly that Budd was misunderstood, that he chastised the media for their portrayal of the forward from Woodbury, N.J. who married his wife, Lois, when he was still in college.

Dave Budd, left, wasn't all smiles during a game, according to team-mate Billy Packer, right. (Courtesy of Wake Forest Media Relations)

"He's a great kid and I would like to have 10 like him on my team," McKinney said. "Budd has had it rough lately. But I want to tell you fellows one thing, you don't find many saints in the world today. God didn't make everybody perfect. If He did, then there would be no need for coaches or many other things.

"Some of you fellows may not like what I'm going to say, but I think you have misused the press where Dave Budd is concerned. I think you should have given a thought to the boy, his wife and his family before you wrote some of the things you did about him. Sure he has made some mistakes, but we all make mistakes.

"If you don't realize it, I want you to know he is a wonderful kid and one of the best basketball players I have had the pleasure of coaching."

Budd played five years for the New York Knicks of the NBA, averaging 7.1 points and 4.6 rebounds a game. He retired in 1965 to take over his father-in-law's wholesale grocery business.

Members of his family donated money to Wake Forest to build the current practice facility in the Miller Center on campus, which is today known as Dave Budd Gym. It has basketball goals, but not a boxing ring in sight.

The Man They Loved to Hate

Few men cut a wider swath through the ACC than McGuire, the legendary coach at North Carolina and South Carolina. McGuire inspired strong passions, for him and against him.

On the subject of McGuire, there was no room for neutrality.

Greason Jr.'s first close encounter with McGuire came during the championship game of 1953 Southern Conference season. Wake Forest, coached by Greason's father, was playing N.C. State for the title, and McGuire, whose Tar Heels had been eliminated, was sitting next to Greason's mother Lib.

"It was a very close game and she was just completely wrung out," Greason Jr. recalled. "McGuire was very conciliatory, gentlemanly and so forth.

"He assured her we were going to win, that he was an expert and that was the flow of the game. And sure enough we did win (71-70)."

Greason Jr. drew a distinctly different impression of McGuire about five years later while serving as Wake Forest's student manager. The Deacons were playing North Carolina in Woollen Gym in Chapel Hill, and Greason Jr., as was the custom of managers of the day, was keeping the visiting team's scorebook.

An official's whistle stopped second-half play, and a foul was called on Murdock. The manager for North Carolina keeping the home book notified the officials that Murdock's foul was his fifth. Greason Jr. counted Murdock's fouls, and came up with only four.

"The referees come and they're talking to us, and we're both firm in our positions," Greason Jr. said. "McGuire came over, faced the scoring table, looked up at the crowd, shot his cuffs, like he often did, straightened his beautiful tie, and said, 'What the expletive, expletive is going on here? You know it's five fouls.'

"He cursed me and so forth. Of course the crowd thought he was just Handsome Frank McGuire."

Greason Jr., sticking to his guns, suggested that the officials send an emissary to press row to see how many fouls the media had recorded on Murdock. Word returned that the foul was, indeed, only Murdock's fourth, and play resumed with Murdock still in the game.

"Frank cursed me again and shot his cuffs again and went back to his bench," Greason Jr. said.

Budd and the Big O

Budd, whose ability to handle himself in a fight is far better remembered than his ability to handle a ball, usually wasn't one to pull his punches. But for one of college basketball's early black stars, Oscar Robertson, Budd made an exception.

Just after Christmas in 1958, early in his junior season, Robertson traveled with his Cincinnati Bearcats to play in the eight-team Dixie Classic at N.C. State's Reynolds Coliseum. The Bearcats' first-round opponent was a rebuilding Wake Forest team still one year removed from ACC prominence.

The Bearcats thumped the Deacons 94-70, but not before push came to shove between Robertson and Budd.

Budd's recount was as follows:

"Robertson tripped me as we started up court a few minutes before the scuffle. I guess both our tempers were building up to a hot point.

"Then under the basket, we got tangled up in a scramble for a rebound and that was it. We fell to the floor and I was on top. I could have hit him, but I didn't. I happened to think about his race, and I knew if I hit him it would cause a lot of trouble.

"If it had been any other player, no one would have thought too much about it. But because of his race, I guess it will look bad for this section (of the country). It's a shame because he is a great player."

Robertson, for his part, shrugged off the incident.

"We went up for a rebound and I came down on his back," Robertson was quoted as saying. "It wasn't anybody's fault. It was just one of those things."

None of which is to say a warm and fuzzy feeling enveloped the proceedings. Afterwards Budd and Robertson declined to shake hands.

"I don't shake hands during or after a game," Robertson explained. "I shake hands before the game."

Fleeing South Carolina at Breakneck Speed

McKinney, in the parlance of the 1960s and 1970s, was a real trip. Some of the best evidence of that came on trips McKinney and his Deacons made back when college basketball teams crisscrossed the rural two-lane highways and byways of America in large, touring automobiles.

The Deacons, during the 1950s, would usually travel in two or three cars, one of which was a 1952 Cadillac limousine the players christened "The Black Mariah." In February of 1959, Greason Jr., the Deacons' senior manager, found himself piloting the Black Mariah across South Carolina in hell-bent pursuit of McKinney.

Wake Forest began its swing through the southern reaches of the ACC by losing at Clemson 58-51 on February 23. The Deacons played South Carolina in Columbia the next night, and although Greason Jr. remembered Wake Forest losing to the Gamecocks, the annals actually recorded a 60-53 victory.

Yet something about the game, be it the fans, the officials, the play of his team—or a combination of all of the above— ticked off McKinney so bad that he pulled out of Columbia at such breakneck speed that Greason Jr. found himself barely keeping up.

"I had Jerry Steele and Dave Budd and somebody else in there and they said, 'Don't you dare lose him. He forgot to give out the meal money,'" Greason Jr. recalled.

Before the caravan could reach the outskirts of Columbia, Greason Jr. was pulled over by a policeman.

"Here comes the blue light," Greason Jr. said. "Bones stops. He sees the problem. He comes back and talks the cop out of giving us a ticket."

Once out on the open road, McKinney really put the pedal to the metal of the station wagon he was driving.

"We were rocking on down the road going 85 or 90 miles an hour and Bones passes a bus," Greason, Jr. said. "And they're just laying the whip to me, not to lose him. So I passed that bus going 90 miles an hour.

"I don't know how Bones was out-running that Cadillac. But here comes the blue light again."

This time McKinney never looked back, but instead kept on rolling toward home. It was left to Greason Jr. to roll down his window and face the South Carolina state highway patrolman.

"So I show him my license," Greason, Jr. said. "My father's name was well known. I had the same name. So he got the drift there.

"And he looked back around the car and there was Steele and Budd and he said, 'I don't blame you boys for wanting to get the hell out of South Carolina as fast as you can. But would you do me a favor and hold it down to no more than 80 until you get to the state line?' He gave me my license back and didn't charge me with anything.

"I think we caught up with Bones at a road house at the other side of Charlotte. So we did get our hamburgers."

"Take the Guy from Wisconsin"

The name John Cantwell, a 5-8 guard from Shawano, Wisconsin, who played two seasons of varsity basketball for Duke, has largely been lost in the tides of time. He played 24 games in 1960 and 11 in 1961, and scored a total of 114 points.

Though Cantwell had little impact at Duke, his recruitment by the Blue Devils did have major repercussions for another ACC school some 75 miles to the west. For in 1958, Coach Harold Bradley was trying to decide whether to offer a scholarship to Cantwell, or to another guard from Bethlehem, Pennsylvania, named Billy Packer.

"I was dilly-dallying a little bit," Packer recalled. "I had a chance to visit Colorado and my father tells me, 'You're not going to visit Colorado. Call up the school where you're going to go and that's it.'

"He said, 'Do you want to go to Duke?' And I said, 'That's where I want to go.' So he called Duke. We're sitting at the supper table. I didn't hear the conversation on the other end, but basically what came back to me from my father was, 'They'll be able to let you know in a couple of weeks. They're trying to decide between you and another player.'

"I said, 'Why don't you call them back and tell them to take the guy from Wisconsin? Because I'm going to Wake Forest and play against his ass.' I called up Bones and said, 'I'd like to accept your offer,' right on the spot."

Unbeknownst to Packer, McKinney didn't have a scholarship to offer. He had already committed the five he had available to Len Chappell, Dave Wiedeman, Frank Loeffler, Gene Compton and Charlie Leonard, the older brother of future Deacons star Bob Leonard.

McKinney's dilemma was resolved when Leonard decided to accept an opportunity to play professional baseball instead of attending Wake Forest.

"And that opened up the scholarship," Packer said. "But Bones never told me about that until I got to college."

Packer, a two-time All-ACC Player, became even better known as a national basketball analyst who was been courtside for many of college basketball's greatest games. Packer was in Indianapolis to call Duke's game against UCLA for CBS on November 30, 2002 when he was given cause to remember how he ended up at Wake, Forest, and not Duke.

"I'm walking down the street in Indianapolis and this guy hollered at me," Packer said. "He said, 'Billy Packer can I ask you a question?' And I said, 'Sure.'

"The guy comes over and he's a doctor from someplace, and he said 'Did you ever hear of John Cantwell?' I said, 'Well, there was a Cantwell that went to Duke.' And he said, 'Yeah, that's my partner, and I'm in a medical practice. And he told me a story how he got the scholarship instead of you at Duke.'

"And I said, 'That's absolutely correct.'"

"I Never Met a Kinder-Hearted Guy"

The last and perhaps most lasting memory many people have of Greason was seeing him dancing with McKinney on the court at Reynolds Coliseum, celebrating Wake Forest's jubilant 53-50 victory over North Carolina in the championship of the 1959 Dixie Classic.

McKinney had succeeded Greason as head coach two seasons earlier, and the grand win over the Tar Heels, with sophomores Chappell and Packer helping lead the way, signified the return of the Deacons to ACC prominence.

Greason, who dedicated his adult life to hunting, his dogs, his family and Wake Forest athletics, was thrilled beyond belief.

"Murray grabbled me with both hands, shook 225 pounds like a leaf, and said hoarsely, 'We did it! We did it! Let me get through there,'" wrote sports editor Frank Spencer in the *Winston-Salem Journal*. "So 225 pounds led interference that brought Murray out beside the Deacon bench. He grabbed Bones McKinney and then grabbed the boys."

Sadly, Spencer, a longtime friend of Greason, wrote the words in an obituary. Two days after the championship, while driving alone back to Winston-Salem from a hunting trip in the eastern part of the state, Greason, still in his hunting clothes, drove off the road near Greensboro and didn't survive.

Greason's 1953 four-door Buick was spotted on what was then called I-70 in southeastern Greensboro by a motorist who said the Buick suddenly veered off the road and crashed in the abutment of the Willow Creek Bridge. It was a few minutes before 9 a.m. Dr. Allan B. Coggeshall, medical examiner of Guilford County, said Greason had suffered a blow to the head.

An assistant director of athletics at Wake Forest at the time, Greason was 58.

For a number of hours, confusion reigned while those who loved Greason attempted to sort out the facts. Although the Deacons beat North Carolina on December 30, and the accident didn't occur until January 1, many people mistakenly remember Greason dying the morning after the championship.

"That morning after we left Raleigh, after the Dixie Classic, the telephone rang and I answered," said Francis, the longtime publicist for Wake Forest and the ACC. "Earl Hellen from the *Greensboro Record* said, 'Skeeter, Bones was killed in an automobile accident.'"

"I said, 'When?' And he said, 'This morning.'

"And I said, 'Where?' He said, 'Well, here in Greensboro.'

"I said, 'No, Bones didn't get killed, because we came back last night after the game.'

"And he said that somebody had called him and told him there was an accident there and the Wake Forest basketball coach was killed. It was Murray.

"He was coming back by himself and ran into that bridge abutment. We all said at the time, 'He went to sleep,' because we all remembered how easily he could go to sleep. We just felt that's what happened."

The Wake Forest community, understandably, was crushed. Greason was a three-sport star at Wake Forest who won 12 varsity letters and was captain of the basketball and football team. He coached Wake Forest's basketball team for 23 years, winning 288 games and losing 243.

And he was a slow-talking, twinkle-eyed man loved by those lucky enough to know him.

"He was one of the most unselfish men in the world and had as many friends as any man I ever knew," McKinney said. "I can't tell you how good he was to me.

"I never met a kinder-hearted guy in my life."

Chapter 3
The Sixties

"With Bones, Every Day Was a Holiday"

A s long as there is an Atlantic Coast Conference—and perhaps even long after, if one could imagine that—fans will
debate over which ACC basketball coach was the absolute greatest and which player was the hands-down best.

But if posterity were to ever award the title of the ACC's
Most Colorful Character, the prohibitive favorite would be a
player, coach and television commentator named Horace A.
McKinney.

Only everybody knew him as Bones.

"With Bones, every day was a holiday and every meal was
a feast," said Charlie Bryant, McKinney's assistant coach.

A wired and wiry 6-6 ball of fire, McKinney was all things
to all people from the time he showed up as a player at N.C.
State in 1941 until he retired from his job as a color analyst in
the 1980s.

To his teammates at N.C. State, and after World War II,
at North Carolina, he was a valued teammate skilled and accom-

plished enough to earn All-Southern Conference honors at both schools.

To the followers of Wake Forest basketball, he was the coach who pulled the program out of the doldrums of the late 1950s and directed the Deacons to two straight ACC championships, five straight appearances in the ACC championship and, in 1962, their only trip to the Final Four of the NCAA Tournament of the 20th century.

To the fans, he was a side-splitting sidelines showman whose incessant, often manic, courtside antics will forever remain the stuff of ACC lore.

To his congregation, he was a Baptist minister whose love for life was exceeded only by his love for his Maker.

To his friends and family, he was a beloved, though at times bewildered and bewildering figure who fought and eventually beat the scary grip of substance abuse.

To all those who came of age watching ACC basketball on the Raycom/Jefferson Pilot network, he was the off-beat grandfatherly figure who, while diagramming plays on a backboard, would invariably end up with chalk on his suit coat.

And to anybody who heard him speak, he was one of the most naturally funny people to ever live. Skeeter Francis, a long-time publicist with Wake Forest and the ACC, often said that McKinney was the kind of speaker who could tell the same joke to the same audience 100 times and have everybody laughing harder on the 100th rendition than the first.

"He'd have that Tipoff Club and they'd meet over at Staley's Restaurant," Francis said. "He'd tell the same stories every week and everybody would just laugh like hell. They were funny. But only Bones could tell them. I could tell you the same story and you'd sit there and think, 'This isn't funny.'

"He told a story, I know 10,000 times, how when he came back in his next life he wanted to be male cheerleader, so he could hold the female cheerleaders up.

"He'd tell that story everywhere he went and they'd just die laughing."

But Maurice George, who played for Wake Forest when McKinney was an assistant to Coach Murray Greason, said it would be a mistake to consider McKinney nothing more than a sideshow clown. He was also, George recalls, a natural coach.

"He was a giant," George said. "He was a giant not only in stature, but he commanded your attention because you knew right away he was knowledgeable. He could get you fired up.

"It's really hard to describe, other than the fact that when you went out on the court, and got ready for the tip, you knew you were as prepared as you could be."

Recruiting Raid

By the time McKinney succeeded Greason as Wake Forest's head coach following the 1957 season, there was ample evidence McKinney knew how to coach and he knew how to motivate.

Two years later, there was even more evidence that not even McKinney could make chicken salad out of chicken feathers.

His first season, during which he won six games and lost 17, convinced him he needed some better players. His second season, during which the Deacons finished 10-14, convinced him he needed them fast.

The Deacon fortunes turned decidedly for the better on one visit McKinney happened to make back home Durham, where he visited Harold Bradley, the Duke coach, at Bradley's office in Duke Indoor Stadium (later to be named Cameron Indoor Stadium). During that visit, Bradley made the grievous mistake of leaving the room without wiping his blackboard clean.

For on that blackboard were two names McKinney had never heard of, but would soon come to know very well. One was Len Chappell. The other was Billy Packer.

"Posted on a blackboard were the names of guys who Duke was recruiting," Packer recounted years later. "They had

Chappell's and Packer's names up and that's how he contacted us.

"That was his story. He always said that's how he got our names."

McKinney convinced both Chappell and Packer to attend Wake Forest. Duke's loss was the Deacons' great gain.

Chappell, a powerful 6-8 center from Portage, Pennsylvania, averaged 24.9 points and 13.9 rebounds over his three seasons of varsity eligibility, was named first-team All-ACC all three seasons and ACC Player of the Year twice, and in 1962 became Wake Forest's first consensus All-American. Packer, a feisty 5-10 guard from Bethlehem, Pennsylvania, averaged 14.8 points over his three seasons of eligibility, played point guard for the first (and through 2004, only) Deacon team to reach the NCAA Tournament's Final Four, and was named second-team All-ACC in 1960 and first-team in 1961.

Wake Forest, during the three seasons Chappell and Packer played varsity basketball, won 62 games and lost 27.

Return of the Conquering Heroes

McKinney liked to win and he liked to party. But most of all he liked to win and then party.

Packer recalled the time in 1960 when the Deacons returned to Winston-Salem from a highly gratifying 80-69 victory at North Carolina. Then only a sophomore from Bethlehem, Pennsylvania, Packer said he didn't understand the significance of beating the Tar Heels in Chapel Hill, and neither did his sophomore teammate Chappell.

"When we got back to the campus it was late obviously, and all the lights were off and everything," Packer said. "We started to trudge out of the bus and get our equipment and that kind of stuff, and all of a sudden Bones said, 'Get your asses back on the bus. This is no way for a school to greet the winners.'"

McKinney ordered the bus driver to pull over to the women's dormitory.

"He started beeping the horn and screaming and hollering," Packer said. "He got everybody up, and hell he rallied the whole student body over in front of the gym.

"In about an hour's time we just went to bed and he was carrying on with his Pepsis, and having a barnstormer there."

Fashion Statement

Tall and gaunt with a scarecrow of a body that clothes just hung on, McKinney was never what one would call a slave to fashion. He was, however, a slave to superstition, which helped explain the red socks he wore while coaching his Deacons.

"I wore them two games in a row during Dave Budd's senior year (1960)," McKinney said. "We won both games. I believe it was against Davidson and State. Then I left them off one game (against George Washington) and we lost.

"Budd told me then I'd better keep on wearing them. That's the way it started."

So insistent was McKinney in not disrupting what he perceived to be the natural order of the cosmos, that once, when he wore conventional black socks to a game, he made a desperate call to his house. His daughter, Kay, rushed the red socks to him in time for tipoff.

And not just any red socks, mind you, would do.

"I started off with just one pair, but everyone has started sending me red socks and I have a pile of them now," McKinney said. "But they have to be a certain kind. If they don't have ribs in them, they're no good."

McKinney became so associated with his red socks that the student government decided to make a little money on the side by selling red socks at games.

"*Pussycats*"

McKinney long remembered 1960 as the year his first championship at Wake Forest got nipped in the Budd.

The Deacons played in their first of five straight ACC championships that season against a Duke team that had stunned heavily favored North Carolina in the semifinals. Even without Dave Budd, his star forward, McKinney felt supremely confident going against the 14-10 Blue Devils.

"We would have beaten the hell out of Duke without Budd," McKinney maintained.

Commissioner James Weaver had declared the infamously combative Budd ineligible against Duke after Budd's fight with Anton Muehlbauer in the semifinal against N.C. State. The conference's executive committee overruled Weaver, however, and Budd was cleared to play at 5 p.m., three hours before tipoff.

McKinney warned Budd of what to expect from the crowd at Reynolds Coliseum.

"When they called his name, they threw that spotlight on him and (the fans) started to boo," McKinney recalled later. "Then they started to applaud, then they gave him a standing ovation. We were 20 points better than Duke, but that made pussycats out of us. Pussycats."

Budd played well, finishing with 10 points and 15 rebounds. But the Blue Devils, getting 22 points from Doug Kistler and 14 from Howard Hurt, upended the Deacons 63-59. It pained Wake Forest to know it had beaten Duke twice that season, 80-63 in Winston-Salem and 83-64 in Durham.

The ruling by Weaver, a former director of athletics at Wake Forest, was influenced by previous dealings with Budd. The year before the ACC had put Budd on strictest probation, the penalty being expulsion from the league, following his role in probably the wildest fight to take place ever in Winston-Salem's Memorial Coliseum.

The opponent, as might be expected, was North Carolina. Late in the game, won by the Tar Heels 75-66, hostilities broke out when Lee Shaffer of North Carolina got into a tussle for the ball with the Deacons' Bill Cullen and Charlie Forte. One thing led to another, which led Budd to wade into the fray and, according to eyewitnesses, pick Shaffer up by the neck and throw him to the floor.

The benches cleared, fights broke out everywhere, McKinney got knocked to the floor, Coach Frank McGuire of North Carolina was cracked on the head and Doug Moe of the Tar Heels emerged with a black eye, courtesy of a fan.

Even reserve forward Winston "Twig" Wiggins, considered one of the mildest mannered of all Deacons, got caught up in the brouhaha. But when he did, his wife rose from her seat behind the Wake Forest bench, walked to courtside and demanded "Winston, you get out of there right this minute."

Weaver, upon a review of game film, censured McKinney and McGuire and reprimanded Forte, Wiggins and Dickie Odom of Wake Forest and Shaffer and Lou Brown of North Carolina with probation. But he really lowered the boom on Budd, ruling that any subsequent on-court altercations would result in the termination of his eligibility.

Furthermore Weaver ruled that Wake Forest's home game against North Carolina in 1960 could not be played in Winston-Salem. Wake Forest officials and fans protested vehemently, and a protest followed in which Weaver's effigy was burned in public.

But Weaver's ruling, in this case, stood, and the Tar Heels beat Wake Forest 62-59 the next season in Greensboro.

Homesick, and Then Some

Though McKinney is rightfully credited with recruiting Jerry Steele to Wake Forest, it took a timely kind word or two from the president of the college, Harold Tribble, to keep Steele in school.

As a freshman recently arrived from the small town of Elkin in the fall of 1957, Steele was tremendously uncomfortable at Wake Forest. He was beyond homesick. He was miserable, so miserable he had already decided to pack up and head home.

Enter Dr. Tribble.

"I was so unhappy," Steele recalled. "One Sunday after church I had decided to go home.

"I was standing in the cafeteria line, waiting for lunch, when Dr. Tribble came by. He stopped and spoke to me. I felt that if the president of a college could stop and speak to a freshman, Wake Forest must be a pretty good place.

"So I stayed."

McKinney had plenty of reasons to thank Tribble. The 6-8, 220-pound Steele, despite averaging just 3.3 points and 3.1 rebounds during his three varsity seasons, provided the frontcourt depth McKinney's teams needed to finally turn the corner and win 21 games in 1960 and 19 games in 1961.

Steele showed great courage as a senior. Playing all season on a bum knee that was injured during a preseason collision with Chappell, Steele still managed to get into 26 of the Deacons' 30 games. His season took another turn for the worse in a first-round NCAA Tournament game against St. John's when a blow from Redman Leroy Ellis caught him in the face, breaking a bone.

"I wasn't a good player, not really," Steele said. "When Len Chappell came in as a center there wasn't much for me to do but move to forward.

"I have been called a hatchet man and maybe that is a fair assumption. But I didn't realize I was a hatchet man. Maybe it's not so much what you are, but what you think you are."

Chair Man of the ACC

Many ACC coaches over the years have had run-ins with officials, fans, opposing coaches and at times even opposing players. McKinney, in his memorable eight-year stint as Wake Forest's head coach, took the art of confrontation one step further. McKinney had a battle with a chair.

Incensed over an official's call during the 1960 Dixie Classic, McKinney broke one of the chairs that helped form the Deacons' bench. A few days later he received a bill from N.C. State, the host of the Tournament, for $14.33 to replace the chair.

Of course, $14.33 back in 1960 would have bought a lot of Pepsis, so McKinney wasn't about to pay up. Instead he had the chair repaired, and painted the colors of Wake Forest and N.C. State—Gold and Black on top and Red and White on the bottom. Everett Case, the coach at N.C. State, agreed that whichever team won a game should keep the chair as a trophy until the next meeting.

The ritual lasted until Case retired during the 1964-65 season. Incidentally, McKinney was usually able to keep an extra piece of furniture around his office those days. Of the 12 games played for the extra stakes, Wake Forest won nine.

Case actually coached the 511th and final game of his career at N.C. State against Wake Forest in Winston-Salem on December 5, 1964. Afterward, a visibly tired Case was overheard to say, "I had to get a chair and sit down."

As it turned out, McKinney had a chair to offer. The Deacons, in Case's final game, beat the Wolfpack 86-80.

"We shook hands just before our game in Winston-Salem in December, 1964," McKinney recalled later. "Everett's hands were livid and ice cold. I asked him if he was feeling all right. Everett replied: 'I just feel so poorly, I don't think I can coach any longer.'"

Case retired the next day, turning the team over to Press Maravich, his chief assistant. Case died of cancer in March, 1966.

The Genius of Bones

Dig deep enough beneath the yarns, stunts, wisecracks and occasional tomfoolery of McKinney, and one could find as keen a basketball mind as the Atlantic Coast Conference has ever known.

"He almost knew too much basketball," said Murray Greason Jr., the son and namesake of the Wake Forest coach who hired McKinney as an assistant. "Because in the timeout huddle he would cover 10 or 12 ideas about what we needed to change or do. And the guys couldn't absorb over about three."

Yet there was one timeout huddle in the middle of the 1960 season when McKinney might as well have recited the Gettysburg Address to his team, for all the attention he was paid. The Deacons, huge favorites, were in a tussle at Memorial Coliseum with Maryland, and, with only seconds remaining, Bones's team was in serious trouble.

"Maryland starts knocking everything in and they were right on the verge of having the upset of the year," recalled Bryant, an assistant coach for McKinney. "They had us down by one point with about six or eight seconds to go and we had a timeout at mid-court. And Bones told Billy Packer to drive down the middle and if he was able to get his jumpshot, take it.

"If he couldn't, he was to try to pass it off to Dave Budd or Len Chappell underneath."

Packer began his drive, but Chappell, for reasons of his own, barged from beneath the basket, took the ball from Packer, turned and nailed the shot just before the buzzer for a 65-64 Wake Forest win.

McKinney was basking in the victory when Carlton Byrd, the sports editor of the *Twin City Sentinel*, approached with a request.

"Carlton wanted Bones to design the game-winning play," Bryant explained. "Bones goes up to the blackboard and draws this play and Carlton takes a picture of it with his camera, and he ran it in the paper the next day."

McKinney told Bryant that he wasn't about to tell the media he had next-to-nothing to do with the game-winning strategy. But careful examination of the play that ran in the *Twin City Sentinel* might have given McKinney away.

For on the blackboard, there for all the readers to see, McKinney had diagrammed not five, but six, Wake Forest players.

Road Kill

Wake Forest has endured its share of killer road trips over the years. It's safe to say that few have been more murderous than the swing through Toledo and Dayton in late January, 1960.

Toledo was ranked No. 13 and Dayton No. 19, while Wake Forest, 11-4 at the time, had slipped from its high-water mark of eighth in the nation to No. 20.

The trip started off badly, with a 70-63 loss to Toledo, and then got worse. Much, much worse.

Dayton was lying in wait for Wake Forest. The Flyers had lost the season before at Wake Forest 66-57, where they felt they had been jobbed by the home officials. And just a month before their trip to Dayton, the Deacons had beaten the Flyers 61-50 in Raleigh in the semifinals of the Dixie Classic.

The Deacons, upon arrival, were confronted by the wildest scene McKinney said he had ever witnessed. The arena was packed, so packed that fans were hanging from the rafters.

Fist fights were breaking out all over, and the game hadn't even started.

Desperate times call for desperate measures, so McKinney decided to hold the ball against Dayton, a team known for its half-court zone. The strategy had worked famously well a month earlier against North Carolina in the Dixie Classic, and helped the Deacons upend the Tar Heels 53-50 for the title.

Bones's move proved, however, to be a highly unpopular strategy with the Dayton fans.

Wake Forest won the opening tap and Budd, the star forward, stood with the ball under his arm at half-court. Much to McKinney's chagrin, the officials never warned the Flyers to abandon their zone and force action, as was required by the rules of the day.

So the Deacons stalled throughout the first half. Guards Packer and George Ritchie eventually became so bored they began calling numbers for plays off the top of their heads and circling through the Dayton defense before returning to half-court.

The movements confused center Len Chappell, who hadn't heard of such plays. Catching the drift, Chappell began calling his own plays.

Eventually Dayton grabbed control of the game and began laying it on Wake Forest. The fans continued to throw trash and debris at his bench, so McKinney sent all of his players who weren't in the game back to the showers with six minutes to go.

Before long a Wake Forest player fouled out, and an assistant coach was rushed to the locker room for a substitute. Winston "Twig" Wiggins came running out to the court, still pulling the jersey over his head.

While waiting for Wiggins's appearance, McKinney, having been assessed a technical, climbed into the stands to sit with the fans. Playing, as always, to the crowd, McKinney blew kisses and grabbed his tie and pulled it above his head, as though he were hanging himself. At some point during all the hubbub, he tossed a cup of water over his shoulder, drenching the fur worn by a woman sitting behind him.

Hardly mollified by their team's 62-45 victory, the angry fans congregated outside the visiting lockerroom chanting "We want Bones. We want Bones."

Inside, huddled with his team, McKinney was ashen.

"Boys, it sounds like they're really mad at us," McKinney said.

From the back of the room came the observation, "It sounds to me, Coach, that they're not mad at us. It sounds like they're mad at you."

Finally state police appeared to escort the Deacons to their bus. Still pelted by insults, rocks and debris, the Deacons hunkered down on the floor while their bus pulled away from the arena on their way home from the road trip across the River Styx.

Opening Closed Doors

Long before it was fashionable, McKinney displayed his social consciousness in his dealings with sportswriter Mary Garber.

Garber, the legendary reporter with the *Twin City Sentinel* and later the *Winston-Salem Journal*, had been covering Wake Forest for more than a decade when McKinney became head coach before the 1958 season. But she had always done so at a distinct disadvantage.

While the locker rooms of the day were opened wide for her male counterparts, Garber was forced to wait outside if she wanted to catch a coach or player for comment. McKinney wouldn't stand for the injustice.

"I've been unfair to you," Bones told Garber. "It's not right for me to hold my conference in the dressing room when

you can't come in. From now on, I promise you that I will hold
my conference outside the dressing room."

He kept his promise, and before long other coaches
around the ACC were following McKinney's lead.

Close Long-Distance Call

Packer, during his playing career at Wake Forest, slipped into
McKinney's office one day and made a long-distance call to
his wife-to-be Barbara, who at the time was attending nursing
school in Philadelphia. While whispering sweet nothings over
the phone, Packer heard McKinney's unmistakable footsteps
clomping down the hall.

"Hold on just a minute," Packer whispered, and he quickly slid underneath the coach's desk.

McKinney entered the room, sat down at his desk and
perused his mail. Never one to sit for long, McKinney rose and
loped out of the room.

Packer poked his head out, looked around, climbed back
into the coach's chair and resumed his conversation.

Wake Forest's Great Chappell

There's a temptation, in looking back through the smoky
prism of history, to compare the relationship of Packer and
Chappell to that of George and Lennie in Steinbeck's *Of Mice
and Men*. And the analogy is not totally misleading.

For there was a lot of the street-wise, discerning George in
Billy, and, at times, a little bit of the halting, gullible Lennie in
Len.

"Packer was the ring-leader of that bunch," recalled
Bryant, an assistant coach. "He led them around. If Packer

Coach McKinney, standing, stole recruit Len Chappell out from under Duke. Chappell, kneeling, went on to become Wake Forest's first consensus All-America player. (Courtesy of Wake Forest Media Relations)

wanted something, he would always have Len upfront to do the dirty work.

"And they generally got it."

But to dismiss Chappell as some lumbering oaf with no mind of his own is to wildly miss the mark. There was far more to the man who in 1962 became Wake Forest's first consensus All-American and led the Deacons to their only Final Four appearance of the century.

"Len was a sharp guy," said Bryant. "Everybody thought Len was a dummy. He wasn't. He was very sharp.

"But Len was just a dynamite player. He had the best touch for a big husky guy I've ever seen."

The accomplishments of Dickie Hemric notwithstanding, the argument can be made that Chappell was the greatest Wake Forest player to be born on the U.S. mainland. Tim Duncan, it should be noted, was born in the Virgin Islands.

Though eligible for varsity competition only three seasons, Chappell closed the 20th century ranked third at Wake Forest (behind Hemric and Randolph Childress) with 2,165 points and third with 1,213 rebounds. He averaged 17.4 points and 12.5 rebounds as a sophomore, 26.6 points and 14.0 rebounds as a junior and 30.1 points and 15.2 rebounds as a senior.

More than 40 years later, no other ACC player had ever averaged 30 points in a season.

He also shot 50.7 percent from the floor for his career, an impressive feat given his surprising range.

"In those days 6-8 was pretty tall for a center," Packer said. "But he weighed 255 pounds and it was all solid, and he was an incredible shooter. And he had really good speed and he was a great rebounder—although he was not a great jumper. He had terrific hands.

"He was not a playmaker, and he was not a finesse player, but he could shoot and he could rebound and he could score and he could shoot from inside and outside. And he more than held his own defensively. He was by far and away the best big man in the league."

And he was always best, Bryant remembered, when it mattered most.

"Every year he would start out in December and he would average about 17 or 18 points," Bryant said. "And then in January, he would be at about 20, 22 or 25. Then by February and March he was in the 30s.

"He would get better every year from December to January to February to March."

Bones, the Family Man

Raising six children is hard work, even for a man who is not juggling careers in coaching and the ministry. But whenever possible, McKinney involved his family in his work.

On Wake Forest road trips, McKinney would take his wife Edna and at least some of their children along. Bryant said the McKinney's room would be crowded with roll-away cots, baby bottles, diapers and clothes.

During the summer, McKinney would combine recruiting trips with the family vacation. And if there were a revival in the area, McKinney might drop in and preach there as well.

Kenny, McKinney's younger son, was a fixture at practices and games. Once, after a particularly appalling performance, McKinney stunned his son by lighting into his team using particularly heated and graphic language.

Later McKinney pulled his son out of earshot of his team.

"I'm not really mad," McKinney explained. "I have to talk to them that way so they'll play good."

So when the time came for McKinney to once again lay down the law to the Deacons, Kenny, without so much as a blink of the eye, turned to Jack Budd, a team manager.

"Daddy's not really mad," the child explained. "He just talks that way so they'll play good."

Bones Flips Them Off

McKinney, a shoo-in for most colorful personality ever in the ACC, had a peculiar problem of keeping his shoes on his feet. There are two classic stories resulting from McKinney kicking his feet in such a way that a shoe flew off into history.

The most famous occurred in perhaps the most famous basketball arena of the day, Kentucky's Memorial Coliseum, where the benches were along the baseline. McKinney kicked at a call during a game against Princeton in the first round of the 1963 Kentucky Invitational, and his shoe sailed off his foot and landed on the playing court. Fortunately, the ball was at the other end.

As Bones slinked out and leaned over to retrieve his shoe, his pens and pencils fell from his shirt pocket and rattled around the floor. He luckily managed to collect his belongings and get back to the bench before the ball changed hands.

When asked later what would he have done if confronted with a Princeton fast break while still on the court, McKinney was quick with his reply.

"I would have played defense," McKinney said, crouching, his long arms flapping.

McKinney also flipped his shoe off once at Philadelphia's Palestra, in a game against St. Joe's. McKinney's good friend, Jack Ramsay, coached St. Joe's, and the two teams played eight times during McKinney's eight seasons as the Deacons' head coach.

The fans at the Palestra delighted in McKinney's antics, and greeted him with great enthusiasm on the Deacons' next trip north to play St. Joe's.

A masked student emerged from the stands wearing a black uniform with a skeleton painted on the front. For a cape, he wore a towel with the letters B-O-N-E-S stenciled down the center. He carried a giant cardboard shoe and presented it to McKinney, who lifted the mask to reveal a grinning face.

Larger Than Life

Before he was a math professor at Wake Forest, and before he became the school's faculty athletics representative, Richard Carmichael played basketball at Wake Forest. A member of the varsity during the 1962, 1963 and 1964 seasons, Carmichael had the honor and pleasure of playing for McKinney.

To this day, any mention of McKinney brings a smile to Carmichael's kindly face.

"You can say pretty much anything you want about Bones," Carmichael said. "And if it wasn't true, it could have been."

McKinney made a similar impression on a writer named Robert Lipsyte, who covered the Deacons' 78-73 victory over St. Bonaventure in Charlotte in the second round of the 1961 NCAA Tournament. Wake Forest had advanced by beating St. John's three days earlier in New York City. The Deacons' win against St. Bonaventure lifted them into the championship of the East Regional, where their road to the Final Four was derailed by St. Joseph's, coached by McKinney's good buddy Ramsay.

The box score of the Deacons' victory over St. Bonaventure did not credit McKinney with an assist. According to Lipsyte, it should have.

"Bones is a tall, skinny man who looks like a Baptist minister, which he is," Lipsyte wrote. "Like a grotesque marionette, he had been jerking up and down off the Deacon bench, his shoulders shuddering, his face twisting into distorted masks. Then he made his move toward immortality.

"An official was holding the ball under the basket, waiting for the players to fan out. McKinney grabbed the ball out of his hands and tossed it to one of his players, who drove down the court and scored."

Packer, the point guard on the team, later described Lipsyte's account as close to accurate. McKinney, according to Packer, actually whipped the ball to Packer, who had barely stepped out of bounds. Packer then hit a breaking Alley Hart for a layup.

McKinney, who had a sign in the den of his home that read, "I'm just a basketball coach, but the rest of my family is normal," would always insist that none of his courtside antics were calculated or choreographed.

"They're really part of me," McKinney said. "I never made up anything or planned it in advance. I guess it's just a spontaneous expression of my feelings. I realize these actions can be detrimental if carried too far. And there have been times when I went too far. But I never meant to blast anyone or make anyone look bad."

Saving a Life, Saving a Soul

McKinney lost his share of games as a player and coach. That's a fate everyone in the arena of competitive athletics has to face.

What McKinney didn't expect to lose, though, was a member of his first congregation as a Baptist minister. And, as he would tell many times later, he came far too close for comfort to doing just that.

McKinney, long after he had retired as a minister and coach, insisted on telling the story of his most harrowing baptism to host Tom Campbell on a television program titled *Dialogue with Bones.*

"We had a lady in there named Mrs. Marshman, and she was close to six feet tall," McKinney recalled. "She was a big woman. One of my members had led her to the Lord. When she was 16 years old she got kicked out of the Methodist Church for dancing, and she just thought she was going to Hell.

"She was a great big lady and you have to be careful in a baptismal pool like that. So I told her, I said, 'Now Mrs. Marshman, don't try to help me.' And I told the last man before her, 'Now you wait over there on the edge of that pool.' And she came in there, and just as soon as I put her under, she raised her feet. And I'm going to tell you, it took me and that guy to get her to stand back up so we could get her out.

"You couldn't laugh, you know. It was too serious for that. (But) it scared me to death. It really did.

"But that was the last one. We had prayer and went home."

Competitive Coat Tossing

Whenever a Wake Forest team coached by McKinney played a St. Joe's team coached by the equally animated Ramsay, the show on the court often paled compared to what was taking place on the sidelines.

McKinney once said there was a good reason he liked Ramsay so much. "Jack was just about as crazy as I was," McKinney explained. During games between the two, Ramsay could as likely as not be found in front of the Wake Forest bench while McKinney was wandering off down in front of the Hawks' bench.

Both were so prone to yanking their coats off and flinging them into the stands, that they actually began keeping score on who could throw theirs farthest. Once, Ramsay's coat sailed a few rows higher into the stands, and McKinney, initially, was a gracious loser.

"It was a great throw," McKinney said. "And it's accurate because it was measured by a priest."

Upon further reflection, McKinney accused his friend and counterpart of foul play. Ramsay, he claimed, had been guilty of "throwing a cheap coat he got at a bargain sale."

McKinney won a rematch when his coat sailed over the crowd at the Palestra and landed on the organist.

McKinney in rare form: fully dressed. The Baptist minister and head coach, known for his antics on the sidelines, often took to tossing his suit coat into the stands or kicking off his shoe in disgust. (Courtesy of Wake Forest Media Relations)

Bones Buckles Up

As many as 250 fans were apt to show up at Staley's Steakhouse in Winston-Salem on Monday afternoon to listen to Coach McKinney pontificate on the state of his basketball team or life in general. At one luncheon, McKinney mentioned that ACC Commissioner Weaver had released an edict stating that coaches would no longer be allowed to jump off their seats on the bench or rail at the officials up and down the sidelines.

"I'm not sure," McKinney wrote in an autobiography titled *Honk Your Horn If You Love Basketball,* "but I think Jim was thinking about me when he announced this new policy."

So McKinney made the mistake of wondering aloud to the luncheon crowd at Staley's if perhaps he needed a seatbelt.

Sure enough, when he showed up to coach his next game, a seatbelt had been installed to his seat—courtesy of what McKinney called his gang at Ammons Esso, a service station the coach regularly frequented.

McKinney, who made it his practice to remain in the locker room until just before tipoff, learned of the prank from his assistant coaches, who asked him if the device should be removed. No, McKinney told them, the publicity of the stunt will far outweigh any embarrassment.

It was a quiet, expectant Memorial Coliseum crowd that watched McKinney walk onto the court and over to his seat. Calmly, without fuss or fanfare, McKinney sat down, and clicked the seatbelt into its holster. A roar welled from the stands and all along press row, flashbulbs popped to illuminate photographs that, the next day, would be published throughout the country.

For about 10 minutes McKinney remained strapped to his seat. After watching a couple of calls go against his team, however, McKinney unbuckled and was back to his old demonstrative self.

McKinney would try to justify his sideline antics by insisting he was only talking to his players, and not riding the officials. Francis, the longtime publicist for Wake Forest and the ACC, said McKinney, in that assertion, was half right.

"Bones, he'd work over the officials pretty good," Francis said. "Bones always said he was talking to his players. And he was. He talked to his players all the time. Bones always said he was never on the officials. But that wasn't true. He got on officials."

Hull and the Void

It will forever be conjecture as to where Wake Forest would have been in 1961 without the contributions of Bill Hull. But McKinney recognized that the Deacons wouldn't be where they ended up, as ACC champions for the first time in school history.

The stars of the 1961 team were Chappell and Packer, but it was Hull who saved the season. When center Bob Woollard and forward Steele were injured during preseason, McKinney talked Hull, an All-ACC end during his college football career, into joining the basketball team.

Hull, a physical 6-6, 220-pound forward from Tarboro, N.C., played in all 30 games, averaging 9.5 points and 9.9 rebounds while shooting 55.3 percent from the floor.

Hull made an early impact, scoring 17 points and pulling down 12 rebounds in the Deacons' 68-67 victory at 10th-ranked N.C. State on December 14.

"Not a bad pickup," McKinney told the sportswriters. "I told Hull after the game that I loved only my wife and children better than him. He was absolutely amazing.

"Before the game, I told him to play like a basketball player, not a football player. And he did, too."

Though drafted by the Chicago Bears of the NFL, Hull cast his lot with the fledging AFL and signed with the Dallas Texans. It was his interception that allowed the Texans to kick the game-winning field goal that beat Houston 20-17 in the 1962 AFL championship game.

The Game of Life

Though immortalized for his outsized personality, unmatched energy and unforgettable antics, McKinney was very much a mortal man.

As such he was susceptible to the same fallibilities we all fight from the time we arrive on earth to the time we leave. For most of the 13 years he was at Wake Forest as an assistant and head coach, McKinney fought the demons he faced every day to at least a draw. He did so with the help of untold quantities of caffeine coursing through his blood from the cases of Pepsi Colas he would consume daily.

Two of the duties of the Wake Forest manager were to keep McKinney stocked in Pepsis, and return the bottles for their deposits. One manager, Tommy Vaughn, who later became a dentist in Rocky Mount, once filled up a Cadillac limousine—trunk, front seat, back seat, even the glove compartment—with bottles and carried them back to Ammons Esso, where the drinks had been purchased.

Asked how many bottles he had, Vaughn replied, "Sixty.

"Sixty cases that is."

By the mid-1960s, with the pressures and demands of preaching on Sunday mornings, coaching a Top-20 college basketball team and raising six children all building up and bearing down on McKinney, Pepsis were no longer enough to get him through the day.

McKinney had been known as a party guy during his NBA career, a chapter of his life he put aside when he first came to Wake Forest to attend the Southeastern Baptist Theological Seminary. But one person who knew McKinney well said Bones made a phone call to a former drinking buddy along about 1964 or 1965.

"'I took my last drink with you about 15 years ago," McKinney told the man. "Come on over here, I'm about to take my next one."

When Bones fell off the wagon, he fell hard. Francis, the long-time publicist for the ACC and Wake Forest said he can remember going to McKinney's house, and helping him carry away the footlocker in which all the beer bottles had been stashed to keep them out his children's sight.

"He got to the place there where really nobody knew him," Francis said. "Nobody knew him.

"He just got tied up with it all."

But just as caffeine wasn't enough, neither was alcohol. To meet the demands of the day, McKinney began taking pills. To erase the demands of the day, McKinney began taking pills of another kind altogether.

"He was living a paradoxical life and it was something that created a lot of internal pressure on him," recalls Bryant, his former assistant coach. "It's something I've been real hesitant talking about, but he had a really tough time.

"What he was doing was he was taking seconals to sleep and amphetamines to keep him awake. That's what they get into."

McKinney would later attribute the brevity of his eight-year career as a head coach to burnout.

"I don't think they called it burnout back then, but that's what it was," McKinney told Ron Morris, the author of *ACC Basketball: An Illustrated History.*

The Deacons, in 1965, finished 12-15 overall and 6-8 in the ACC. Only weeks before the 1966 season began, McKinney was replaced as head coach by Jackie Murdock, his assistant coach and former captain. After one year, Jack McCloskey replaced Murdock.

All lives are, at least to some degree, tragedies, but that of McKinney was not tragic. After leaving Wake Forest, he regained the upper hand on his addictions to become head coach for the Carolina Cougars of the ABA and later a popular commentator for the early telecasts of ACC basketball. He died in Raleigh on May 16, 1997 at the age of 78, following a stroke.

"He came back and he got all right," Francis said. "He and Edna had this place below Raleigh and a couple of the kids were in the area.

"I was within a mile of his place, and it was a combination pool hall and beer place. I pulled in there and asked the guy behind the bar, 'Does anybody know a friend of mine in this area by the name of Bones McKinney?'

"And the guy behind the bar said, 'I've never heard of him.' I said 'O.K.'"

Behind the Barn

A s director of athletics at Wake Forest during the time, Gene Hooks faced the tough question of what to do with a popular basketball coach who was having troubles in his personal life. The full account of McKinney's substance abuse never became public knowledge during those days, but word obviously leaked out in the Wake Forest community.

One serious point of contention between Hooks and McKinney involved an automobile Wake Forest provided McKinney as part of his financial recompense as head basketball coach. McKinney, unbeknownst to Hooks, had wrecked the car and had it towed up behind a farmer's barn in the countryside outside of Winston-Salem.

"It was a rental car," explained Francis. "That's when he and Hooks were at it, because they couldn't find the car.

"It was up there behind some farmer's barn. It was on the university card. They were sending the bill every month for the rental car, and nobody knew where the car was."

Long's Long and Winding Road

Five college coaches had the privilege of coaching Paul Long. But none of them coached Long for long.

Long, a 6-2 product of Louisville, began his college career playing at Virginia Tech for head coach Guy Strong, who was replaced by Bill Matthews for Long's sophomore season in Blacksburg.

Upon transferring to Wake Forest after the 1963-64 season, Long was forced by NCAA regulations to sit out the 1964-65 season, McKinney's last as the Deacons head coach. Long then played for head coach Murdock as a junior in 1965-66 and for McCloskey as a senior in 1966-67—for a total of five coaches in five years.

Long made the most of his two years at Wake Forest, starring for two otherwise nondescript teams. He ranked second in the ACC to North Carolina's Bob Lewis with an average of 24 points a game as a junior, and second to Duke's Bob Verga with an average of 22.3 points a game as a senior.

He was voted second-team All-ACC as a junior and first-team All-ACC as a senior.

"Unconscious, and I Was"

Nineteen games into his varsity career at Wake Forest, Charlie Davis had given Deacon fans plenty of reason to feel that they had something special in the skinny 6-1 guard from the Bronx.

Davis's 20th game served as confirmation.

The Deacons, having suffered through four straight losing seasons, were one of the surprise teams of the ACC in 1969. Sparked by Davis and Gil McGregor, the school's first prominent black players, the Deacons won 18 games and lost nine and finished tied for third in the ACC with an 8-6 conference record.

On February 15, three days after being pounded 122-93 at Duke for their fifth loss in six games, the Deacons were looking to lick their wounds against nonconference foe American University in Memorial Coliseum. But the Eagles were game enough to weather Davis's 16 first-half points to trail only 49-45 at halftime.

Early in the second half, Davis was fouled hard by Gordon Stiles of American. Davis first got mad, then he got even.

"I remember making a steal and then getting undercut while going in for the layup," Davis said. "Everyone knew I was upset because I would start pounding the ball on the floor and my dribble got higher."

What followed was the most withering barrage on the basket in Wake Forest history.

While a crowd of 3,500 Deacon diehards roared its approval, Davis scored 15 straight Wake Forest points in a span of four minutes and 54 seconds. Davis had 37 points and the Deacons led 80-70.

Davis was hot and his teammates were fanning the flames.

"I remember quite honestly seeing Dickie Walker pass up three or four good shots himself to pass the ball cross-court to me," Davis said. "It got to the point where the crowd was actually keeping count and screaming my point total every time I scored. They kept telling my teammates to get me the ball."

And when he got the ball, Davis knew what to do with it, scoring seven more points in another 44-second flurry that gave him 44 points with three minutes remaining. He was bearing down hard on Chappell's school record of 50 points in a single game.

Fouled with 18 seconds remaining, Davis, an 87.3 percent free-throw shooter for his career, drilled both to run his total to 49 points.

"The crowd was yelling 'You've got 49, you've got 49,'" Davis recalled. "And that's when Bobby Rhoads, my running mate at guard, committed a foul so we could get the ball back one more time."

Davis drove to the basket with 10 seconds left, drew a shooting foul, and made both free throws for 51 points, eclipsing the record Chappell had set against Virginia seven seasons earlier.

Davis, who averaged 22.8 points as a sophomore and 24.9 for his career, scored 35 of Wake Forest's 56 second-half points. For the game, he knocked down 19 of 27 attempts from the floor and 13 of 14 from the free throw line. The Deacons won 105-81, igniting a seven-game winning streak that didn't end until they lost to fourth-ranked North Carolina 80-72 in the semifinals of the ACC Tournament.

"Today they call it 'Being in another zone,' but back then you were 'unconscious,' and I was," Davis recalled years later. "It's easy to look back at that night in retrospect and try to figure out why or how it happened, but all I know is I was playing awfully well."

Chapter 4
The Seventies

"Carl Keeps It More Inside"

When one of your nicknames is "The Great Stone Face," chances are you don't do stand-up comedy for a living.

Coach Carl Tacy of Wake Forest could be downright loquacious when the mood struck him, or when in the company of those he was comfortable with. But many days, taciturn was the best way to describe the introverted, guarded coach with the thick eyebrows and a disarming manner of looking past someone addressing him.

Bob Quincy, a venerable sportswriter with the *Charlotte Observer*, was gathering color on Tacy to liven up an article he was writing. Quincy saddled up next to Mary Garber, the legendary Wake Forest beat writer for the *Twin City Sentinel* and *Winston-Salem Journal*.

"Mary, tell me a funny story about Tacy," Quincy said.

Garber thought about it, but not for long,

"I like Carl," Garber replied. "But I don't know any funny stories about him."

Tacy's distant demeanor became a serious issue in 1983. In the sober aftermath of a late-season 130-89 thrashing by N.C. State in Reynolds Coliseum, members of the team met with Athletics Director Gene Hooks to complain about the lack of communication between the coach and the players.

The Deacons lost to the Wolfpack, the eventual national champions, by just one point (71-70) six days later in the first round of the ACC Tournament, and then won three games in the NIT before losing to Fresno State in the semifinals at Madison Square Garden.

A year later Wake Forest enjoyed one of its most memorable seasons, finishing 23-9 and advancing all the way to the final of the Midwest Regional where the Deacons lost to Houston. By then, the players said the differences were past history.

"He has been more receptive to the players this year," senior guard Danny Young said. "He's made a strong effort to be available to us, and the players have responded to that really well. It has been a very good year, in terms of player-coach relationships.

"Some people think because he's quiet, he's hard to get next to. But he has told the players many times that he loves them. He has been very open with us."

Tacy, true to form, did not publicly address the issue at the time. But a year later he admitted to Tony Barnhart of the *Greensboro News and Record* that it was his wife, Donnie, who helped him through the difficult episode.

"She said, 'Hey, it's not the end of the world—basketball needs you a lot more than you need it,'" Tacy said. "She told me I didn't have any apologies to make with the job I had done. That really helped me. I think it opened up a whole new perspective and outlook.

"I don't think I will ever drive and push myself and punish myself like I have in the past. I just don't think that will take place again no matter what I do. Whatever it is I'm feeling, I think I've graduated from some of the pressures of the past."

It was also easy to misread Tacy's stoicism for acceptance. Hank Norton, the man who hired Tacy to coach at Ferrum Junior College in Virginia, said such an assumption would be mistaken.

"He's as intense as Bobby Knight, although in a different way," Norton said. "Carl keeps it more inside."

Tacy acknowledged his burning competitive drive in an interview with Helen Ross of the *Greensboro News and Record*, only weeks after he had suddenly and unexpectedly retired in June of 1985.

"I miss the competition," Tacy said. "I have always felt that, regardless of what some sportswriters felt, I was a very competitive person.

"You know I have a friend from Florida and we have an ongoing card game. The last time he visited we played cards all through the night—neither of us willing to yield. He was in the lead most of the time, but I wouldn't let him stop until I caught up. I was out to win even at that."

Joy Courtesy of Foye

The mascot of the North Carolina Tar Heels is a ram, which is why you may have heard Wake Forest fans refer to their rivals from Chapel Hill derisively as "The Goats."

And for years, the only two words they needed to really get the goat of The Goats were Lee Foye.

If it had not been for one second in the ACC Tournament of 1973, Foye, a 6-6, 205-pound forward from High Point, would be largely forgotten today. But with one improbable basket, Foye helped spring one of the great upsets in conference history.

Seeded seventh in a seven-team conference with a 3-9 ACC mark, Wake Forest faced second-seed North Carolina in the first round. The Deacons played really well, well enough, in fact, to be in the game at the very end.

But the good college try didn't appear to be good enough when first-year coach Tacy huddled with his team in the last timeout of regulation. Only one second remained, and the Deacons trailed 48-46.

They had the ball underneath the North Carolina basket, 94 feet from their own.

"I had those guys seated on the bench and talked to them about the only thing we could do was to catch it and shoot it in one motion," Tacy recalled. "I talked with Bobby (Dwyer) about making the pass, because he had been in the game and played quite a bit of it. He said, 'Coach I can't make that pass. I've got a shoulder problem.'

"Before I could say anything else, Eddie Payne stepped forward and said, 'Coach, I've got it. Don't worry about it. I've got it.' And that was the difference. That IS the difference in athletic events—you've got somebody who wants the ball and who can make the play, and others who are a little bit doubtful."

The situation called for a hero, and the hero proved to be Foye.

Payne's baseball pass barely cleared the fingers of players gathered around the free-throw line and reached Foye on the baseline. Foye, a freshman who would average only 4.4 points over his four-year career, turned and made the short jumper that sent the game into overtime.

"I made a move from left to right and nobody from Carolina followed me," Foye recalled later. "I remember thinking, 'Hey, I'm going to catch this ball. This is great. Now what am I going to do with it?' I didn't have time to dribble or make a move. I had to throw it up. I heard the buzzer right after I released the shot."

Inspired, the Deacons played the Tar Heels toe to toe in overtime and pulled off the upset when Tony Byers went up for a last-second shot, only to dish off to Phil Perry for a layup as time expired on the Deacons' 54-52 victory.

"Charles, Is It Worth It?"

The day he signed with Wake Forest was a big day in Charlie Davis's life. So was February 15, 1969, the day he set a Wake Forest single-game record by scoring 51 points against American. And so was the day, in 1971, that he became the first African American to be named the ACC Player of the Year.

His selection as the ACC's top player quelled somewhat a controversy that had been raging since the year before, when South Carolina's white star, John Roche, outpolled North Carolina's black star Charlie Scott.

Said Davis later: "When they were getting ready to do the vote, I told them if I didn't win this thing, there'd be no way in the world you can ask anyone to send a black player down here. I was the best player in the conference, no ifs, ands or buts about it."

Still, no day ranked higher on Davis's list than May 21, 1990, the day he graduated from Wake Forest 19 years after leaving the campus as a senior for the NBA. Disappointed in himself because he had failed to earn a degree, Davis took three classes in the spring semester of 1990 to complete his bachelor's degree in English.

On hand for the ceremony were his wife Linda, his daughters Sharrika and Sydney and his mother-in-law, Corinne Phillips.

"I am ecstatic," Davis said. "I am absolutely as proud of myself as I can be, without being egotistical.

"I struggled. There were some nights when I was sitting in the basement at 1 and 2 in the morning studying and I'd ask myself, 'Charles, is it worth it?' Sure, I said that a couple of times. But every time the answer was, 'You're damn right it's worth it.'"

Also present to help Davis celebrate was Billy Packer, who, as an assistant coach more than two decades earlier had helped recruit Davis to Wake Forest. The two remained close over the years.

"After the ceremony, Charlie came to my house and we just started crying together," Packer said. "We just cried right there."

Another favorite day in Davis's life came six years later when Sharrika Davis graduated from Wake Forest. In doing so, she became the first offspring of an African American alumnus to graduate from the school.

Simpson Ollie Brown

Back when he played for Wake Forest in the 1970s, Skip Brown was said to bear an uncanny facial resemblance to Motown's young star, Michael Jackson.

Today, now that he's a bank executive working in Winston-Salem, Skip Brown doesn't look a bit like Michael Jackson.

But then, who does?

Brown never achieved Jackson's fame, or infamy, as the case may be, but many people remember him as one of the ACC's best guards in a day when the league had more of its share of good ones. He averaged 18.8 points a game over his four seasons (1974-77) and made first-team All-ACC as a sophomore and senior and second team as a junior.

Not making first team as a junior was a bitter disappointment for Brown, who had averaged 20.9 points a game while playing much of the season with a bruised kneecap. When Phil Ford of North Carolina, Tate Armstrong of Duke and John Lucas of Maryland were voted to the first team, and Brown was relegated to second team, Brown took umbrage.

"I'm the best guard in the ACC," Brown said in November of 1976, not long before his senior season was to begin. "On one leg last year I was quicker than Phil Ford and Tate Armstrong. I deserve a little more credit than I have been getting."

Skip Brown may have resembled a young Michael Jackson in the face, but on the college court he looked more like a young Michael Jordan. (Courtesy of Wake Forest Media Relations)

Born and raised in Kingsport, Tennessee, Brown was named for his father, Simpson Ollie Brown. But one of his five older sisters, Alma, said she really didn't like the ring of the name Simpson, so she nicknamed her baby brother Skip shortly after he was born.

The University of Tennessee recruited Brown, but wanted him to redshirt as a freshman to preserve his season of eligibility. Brown eventually chose Wake Forest over N.C. State, Virginia Tech and Florida State, mainly because Deacon assistant Larry Williams had been the most tenacious recruiter.

After an impressive freshman season, during which he averaged 13.2 points, Brown really burst onto the national scene with a string of big-time games early in his sophomore season.

Of the many praises the writers sung of Brown, perhaps the most melodious was penned by Bruce Phillips of the *Raleigh Times* with a dateline of Greensboro.

"In a grouping of the best college basketball guards in the world, don't Skip Brown," Phillips began. "Friday and Saturday, in the Big Four Tournament here, the Wake Forest sophomore took his place among the game's grandiose with a performance that should be hanging in The Louvre.

"He wears Skip on the back of his jersey and scoots across the hardwood like a bar of wet soap. He is so quick the only way to stay with him is with a camera. By the time a defender gets to him, he's moved to a new address.

"His shooting range is anywhere inside the city limits. He has amazing body control.

"Skip Brown is the total guard: Leader, shooter, defender, ball handler, inspirer. And his work is almost sleepy effortless perfection that marks all the good ones."

Along about that time, two ACC coaches weighed in on Brown's ability.

One was his own coach, Tacy.

"I don't think any coach likes to feel that his program is built around one player, but there is no way we can measure Skip's value to us," Tacy said. "I said before the season that he was one of the most exciting guards in the country, and it looks like he may be better than even our staff recognized."

Another was Coach Norman Sloan of N.C. State.

"Skip Brown will make Wake Forest fans forget about Charlie Davis," Sloan said.

Though he didn't stick in the NBA, Brown finished his college career with a flourish. With the emergence of power forward Rod Griffin as an inside threat, the Deacons won 22 and lost eight and reached the finals of the 1977 Midwest Regional before losing to Marquette, the eventual national champions, 82-68.

"It Was a Robbery"

Were it not for one call in one ACC Tournament while Wake Forest was playing one particular team, Fred Hikel, a former ACC official, would be mostly forgotten today.

Instead Hikel will live forever in Wake Forest infamy as the ref who made "The scoreboard call."

"It was a robbery," Tacy said almost three decades later. "We were robbed. We were. No question."

The season was 1975, which had started well enough for Wake Forest. The Deacons knocked off 16th-ranked Creighton and then upended N.C. State—breaking the Wolfpack's 36-game winning streak—on the way to their second straight Big Four title.

By the second week of January, the Deacons were ranked in the Top 20 at 8-3, rarefied air indeed for a young team so heavily reliant on sophomores Brown and Jerry Schellenberg and freshman Griffin.

Perhaps the Deacons' inexperience did, indeed, catch up with them; they lost nine of their next 11 and finished the regular season 13-13. In ACC play, they tied with Duke for last at 2-10.

One of the great upsets in ACC Tournament history, then, appeared to be brewing when seventh-seeded Wake Forest led North Carolina, the second seed, by eight points with only 54 seconds remaining.

The Deacons led 90-86 with 33 seconds left when Hikel made the signature call of his career.

During a timeout, Tacy drew up the play that had Schellenberg throwing a home-run pass to Brown over the Tar Heel press. The play worked to perfection and Brown was driving for a basket when he was fouled hard by North Carolina's Dave Hanners. One official, Hank Nichols, was reporting the call to the scorer's table when the other, Hikel, blew his whistle and waved off the play.

Hikel, the trail official, ruled that Schellenberg's high, arching pass had grazed the scoreboard hanging above Greensboro Coliseum. Instead of lining up for two foul shots from Brown—whose career free-throw percentage was 83.6—the Tar Heels received the ball out of bounds under their own basket.

Walter Davis drilled a jump shot, and Brown surprised everybody, most of all himself, by missing the front end of a one and one. Brad Hoffman capitalized with a basket at the buzzer to force overtime.

The Deacons were assessed a technical during overtime for not forcing action against North Carolina's Four-Corners delay, and Hoffman made the free throw that lifted the Tar Heels to a 101-100 victory.

Having dodged the bullet, the Tar Heels, led by freshman Phil Ford, outlasted Clemson in the semifinal and then beat David Thompson and N.C. State for the ACC title.

There are those who have long insisted that Coach Dean Smith of North Carolina convinced Hikel that Schellenberg's pass grazed the scoreboard. But after the game, Smith had another story.

"I didn't see it hit," Smith told the media.

Neither did Schellenberg or Brown, both of whom were incensed by the loss and the way it had transpired.

"I watched the ball all the way down the court and it didn't hit the scoreboard," Schellenberg said. "If it had nicked the scoreboard, the ball wouldn't have kept rotating the same way it had been."

Added Brown: "I had the best view of anybody. It was nowhere close to hitting."

Tar Heel fans can argue until they're Carolina blue in the face that their team has not, over the years, received preferential treatment from the refs in games against Wake Forest. A common Deacon response is summed up in two words: Scoreboard call.

"Of course Fred Hikel never called another ACC game," Tacy said, later. "People in the ACC office had to see it our way.

"We would never have played another game he officiated. If he had been ever assigned to another game, I had made up my mind we would take our team off the floor and not play it."

"You Knew Where He Stood"

Maybe he was preoccupied with the previous night's loss to Duke. Maybe he was thinking about the game his team was about to play against N.C. State in the consolation of the 1975 Big Four Tournament.

Whatever was on his mind, Coach Dean Smith of North Carolina took at least a moment to think of the Wake Forest fan sitting directly behind his team's bench, calmly reading a newspaper.

By way of advance apology, Smith explained to the man that he would likely have his view of the game blocked by the Tar Heels' standing routine of standing to celebrate a teammate's good play.

"That's all right, Coach," Hugh Strickland responded. "I'm just going to sit here and read my paper until the varsity game starts."

Any suspicion Smith may have harbored that he wasn't dealing with an ordinary Wake Forest fan would have been well-founded. From the early 1950s when he adopted Wake Forest as his team because he liked the Deacons' Black and Gold colors, until he passed away on December 3, 2001, Strickland was as devoted and loyal a fan as any college basketball program could ever have.

Strickland, who owned and operated a construction company in Winston-Salem, was devoted and loyal enough to attend 339 straight Wake Forest basketball games. From early in the 1980 season until they lost at Connecticut 84-75 on December 2, 1991, the Deacons didn't play a basketball game that Strickland wasn't there to see.

During that span of 339 games, the Deacons played in Santa Clara, Tuscaloosa, New Orleans, New York, New York again, Jacksonville, Lincoln, St. Louis, Boston, El Paso, Honolulu, Santa Clara again, Philadelphia, Palm Beach, Denver, Albuquerque and Tempe. And every time they took the floor, Hugh Strickland was there to cheer them on.

Though a super fan of the highest order, Strickland wouldn't have been noticed by anyone not looking for him. He didn't scream at the officials. He didn't wave signs at television cameras or poke people nearby with oversized foam fingers. But he showed up. Game after game, Strickland showed up and rooted on his favorite team.

When Wake Forest moved to Winston-Salem before the 1956-57 season, Strickland, who never attended college, walked up to the ticket window at Memorial Coliseum and purchased six season tickets on the front row. By 1958, he was a fixture at Deacon games. Years later he refuted any notion that Bones McKinney, Wake Forest's flamboyant coach, was a showman and little else.

"He was a great coach," Strickland said. "So many times late in a game there would be a timeout, and he would tell the team exactly what the other team was going to do. I know he did, because I was sitting on the front row and could hear him."

In December of 1974, with the Deacons coming off a season during which they finished 3-9 in the ACC, Strickland traveled to Portland to watch Wake Forest play Washington State, Iowa and Creighton in the Far West Classic. He was the only Wake Forest fan from Winston-Salem there, which gave Tacy one more fan from back home than he had assistant coaches. Tacy's two assistants, Neill McGeachy and Larry Williams, were elsewhere on the road recruiting.

Tacy invited Strickland to a meeting of tournament coaches and introduced him as his assistant. Strickland didn't sit on the front row during the tournament. He sat on the bench with the Deacon players.

"Hugh Strickland knew that my nerves were a little bit frayed, and I was having kind of a rough time," Tacy recalled years later. "He had a rented car, and said, 'You need to get away. Let's just go driving.'

"He got me out in the car and it was the greatest thing that could have ever happened because it sort of broke the tension that I had about the games and getting everything done. He was good at that sort of thing. He never got too high or too low, wins or losses. He was very steady and he was a great friend.

"You knew where he stood. He didn't change."

Strickland's consecutive-game streak almost ended at 41. During Wake Forest's game against Boston College in the 1981 NCAA Regional in Tuscaloosa, Strickland began feeling so bad that he found himself at the first-aid station lying next to a man who had just had a heart attack.

The next day, Strickland visited his doctor in Winston-Salem, and the day after that he had his kidney removed because of a malignant tumor. As fate would have it, the Deacons lost to Boston College 67-64 and Strickland recovered well before Wake Forest opened at Richmond the next November.

By the time Strickland's eyesight began to fail him in the early 1990s, Dave Odom, then the Deacons' head coach, had already promised to get Strickland to any game he wanted to attend. Odom said he would have the team bus swing by Strickland's house to pick him up.

Strickland's son, Gary, a 1973 graduate of Wake Forest and team manager, has been the longtime scorekeeper at Wake Forest games. Gary recalled the last game of his father's consecutive-game streak, when the Deacons beat Fairfield 91-62 on November 30, 1991. Afterward, Odom invited Strickland back to the locker room and presented him with the game ball.

Though he never attended Wake Forest, Strickland didn't have to attend 339 straight Deacon games to think like someone who did.

"I've always told Gary that it's wrong to hate anybody," Strickland said. "But I told him, 'If you absolutely have to hate anybody, pick North Carolina.'"

Schellenberg Steps Up

As a senior playing for Floyd Central High School in Floyd Knobs, Schellenberg was runner-up to Kent Benson, the future star for Indiana University, in the voting for Mr. Basketball in Indiana.

Over two nights of basketball in early January, 1976, players from North Carolina and N.C. State could certainly see why.

The Deacons won the Big Four Tournament the year before, but their chances of repeating as champs were severely diminished when Brown, their star point guard, was hurt in the 95-83 semifinal victory over North Carolina.

N.C. State entered the championship game against the Deacons averaging 104 points a game. Instead of trying to control tempo, however, Tacy of the Deacons opted for a fast-break strategy that unleashed the unlikely talents of Schellenberg.

A 6-6, 215-pound junior with the size and mobility of a forward, Schellenberg was nevertheless savvy and skilled enough to flourish as the Deacons' second guard. After scoring 7.5 points in a reserve role as a freshman, he averaged 11.8 points as a sophomore, 15.7 points as a junior and 14.7 points as a senior.

His game came together like never before in the 1976 Big Four. He scored 24 in the semifinal game against North Carolina, then dominated N.C. State with 31 points, four assists, four rebounds and three steals.

He took 17 shots from the floor and drilled 13, as the Deacons, coming off the disappointment of the 13-13 finish of 1975, stunned the ninth-ranked Wolfpack 93-78.

Manna From Heaven

Basketball programs spend thousands of dollars and hundreds of man-hours chasing players capable of keeping them competitive.

And then there are those days, the best of days, when a coach will just open the door and his star will walk in.

Tacy had such a day in the summer of 1973, the first day of his basketball camp. Coming off a season during which his Deacons lost nine of their last 12 to finish 12-15, Tacy needed help.

And help arrived, courtesy of a merchant from Fairmont, N.C. named Linwood Rich.

Tacy noticed the arrival, but didn't recognize the player.

"Here comes this big strapping youth, with arms as big as my legs," Tacy recalled decades later. "I thought he was maybe a counselor who had come. And I was quick to ask him in the hallway if he was one of our counselors.

"He said no, he had come to be a part of the camp as a player."

Carl Tacy meet Rod Griffin.

Griffin, steered to the camp by Rich, a family friend back in Fairmont, was manna from heaven for Tacy, just as Tim Duncan would be for Dave Odom two decades later. A powerful 6-6, 225-pound forward, Griffin cracked the starting lineup in his first week of practice, averaged 18.6 points and 8.9 rebounds for his career, was ACC Player of the Year in 1977 and a year later would become the only Wake Forest player other than Len Chappell to lead the ACC in scoring (21.5 points per game) and rebounding (10 rebounds per game).

Tacy's task was not to recognize Griffin's unmistakable ability, but to keep word of it from leaking out to rival recruiters. Griffin was heading into his senior year at Fairmont, a hamlet of less than 3,000 people about 15 miles south of Fayetteville, eight miles from the nearest major highway and apparently in another world from the experts who follow recruiting.

"Clemson and Maryland sent me their brochures and a letter or two, but they never came to see me," said Griffin, who chose Wake Forest over UNC Charlotte, UNC Wilmington, Campbell and Pembroke State.

Coach Smith of North Carolina came close to catching wind of the force that would soon blow through the ACC. Smith attended a game in North Carolina's Class 2-A Tournament to scout another player. He was approached by Richard Bass, Griffin's coach, who suggested Smith stick around for the next game to watch Griffin play.

Smith nodded, but was gone by the time Fairmont High took the floor. And it probably pained Smith to learn later that Griffin had grown up a Tar Heel fan.

It didn't take Tacy long to realize that Griffin was a special player.

In the ninth game of Griffin's freshman season of 1975, the Deacons beat N.C. State in the semifinals of the Big Four Classic. In doing so, they snapped a 36-game winning streak by the Wolfpack, the defending national champions.

In that game, the great David Thompson went strong to the basket, only to have his shot blocked by Griffin.

Tacy said that Griffin provided Wake Forest the inside presence the program had been sorely lacking. He and his coaches quickly realized that the powerful Griffin was all but unstoppable within 12 to 15 feet of the basket.

Griffin wasn't the only forward Tacy recruited before the 1974-75 season, and he certainly wasn't the most heralded. The recruit that arrived with the most fanfare was Charlie Floyd of Philadelphia.

Funny how things work out. Floyd played two years for Wake Forest, averaging 6.8 points and 4.6 rebounds, before transferring.

Rod Conquers a New World

Basketball was never a problem at Wake Forest for Griffin, the 1977 ACC Player of the Year. He was playing first team the first week of practice and remained a four-year starter.

But for a young man from a small town raised by his grandparents on the modest family farm, the small private university posed another kind of problem in itself.

Griffin's mother moved from their hometown of Fairmont, N.C., to New York City to find work. Griffin remained behind to help out on the farm, read the sports page to his blind grandfather, and, on Sundays, attend First Baptist Church.

So if he wasn't the most worldly or sophisticated student on campus, there was a reason. His coach, Tacy, said that Griffin grew in many ways during his four years at Wake Forest.

"Every day you could see a change in Rod for the better," Carl Tacy recalled years afterward. "He just gained so much confidence, and everybody loved him.

"He was one of the standouts in my mind."

Though a first-round draft choice by the Denver Nuggets in 1978, Griffin was three or four inches shorter than the prototypical NBA power forward. But he did all right by himself and his family by playing many years for the top professional teams in Italy.

Leaping Leroy McDonald

In the next-to-last game of his college career, Leroy McDonald was hot, his team was playing well and the ACC Tournament crowd in Greensboro Coliseum was chanting his name.

McDonald, a junior college transfer, averaged 12.3 points and 5.1 rebounds as a senior at Wake Forest. A 6-5 forward from New York City whose leaping ability defied gravity, McDonald proved to be a nice third option behind Griffin and Johnson on a 1978 team that would finish 19-10 overall.

The day before, with Griffin held to only eight points, McDonald poured in 16 of his 18 points in the first half of the Deacons' 72-61 victory over Virginia. Now the Deacons were playing North Carolina in the semifinals, and McDonald was only getting hotter.

Foul trouble for the Deacons forced McDonald to swing into the backcourt to play guard. No problem. At one point, he was even guarding Phil Ford, the Tar Heels' All-America point guard. No problem. With 1:36 remaining, McDonald scored a key basket off a follow shot and the Deacons upended the top-seeded Tar Heels 82-77.

McDonald scored 21 points against North Carolina, but saved his best moves for later, when he led the Deacons in a victory dance in the locker room.

Though the Deacons lost to Duke 85-77 in the championship, they certainly didn't have McDonald to blame. McDonald burned the Blue Devils for 22 points and 14 rebounds to finish the three-day tournament with a total of 61 points and 29 rebounds.

"The one thing I wanted to do was end up my year strong," McDonald said. "I'm satisfied with the way I played."

A fourth-round selection by the NBA's Buffalo Braves, McDonald played one season of professional basketball in Italy.

Frank Asks For It

Frank Johnson's ebullient personality, broad smile and deadly jump shot—not necessarily in that order—made him one of the most popular Deacons to play in the late 1970s and early 1980s. But there was one day in early 1981 when his approval rating among his teammates took a serious plunge.

Practice was going badly, so badly, in fact, that Tacy blew his whistle in exasperation.

"We're getting nothing done," Tacy lamented. "We'll just come out at 6 in the morning and see if some of this sinks in."

Johnson raised his hand.

"Hey coach, I've got an 8 o'clock class," Johnson said. "How about 5:30 in the morning?"

Tacy had another idea.

"In that case, everybody be here at 5," Tacy said.

The Smiling Deacon

Before he was even a full-grown man, Johnson learned to be his own man. And because of it, the Wake Forest basketball program benefited many times over.

Johnson's brother, Eddie, had been a star at Auburn, and Frank wanted to follow his brother's footsteps to the Plains. His father was also partial to Auburn.

"But my mother, she wanted me to go to Wake Forest," Johnson said. "She wanted me to grow up on my own, to learn to make my own decisions."

*While fans called the popular Frank Johnson "The Smiling Deacon,"
teammates referred to him as "Hollywood" because of his flair for the
dramatic. Both were in agreement on one thing, however: Johnson was
damn good. (Courtesy of Wake Forest Media Relations)*

As badly as he wanted to land Johnson, a high school star in Weirsdale, Florida, Tacy recalled years later that he waited on Johnson about as long as he could afford to wait.

"When we recruited him, he was really late in trying to make a decision," Tacy recounted. "I said, 'Frank, we really want you, but if you don't come pretty soon I'm going to go ahead and recruit other guards. Does that make any difference to you?

"He said, 'No Coach, I don't care who you get. If I come, I'm going to play.' That was his attitude. It didn't matter who was there.

"As a coach, that was an attitude that you hope that your players will have, and you try to recruit. More times than not they're going to be the same type all the way through, and they can do some great things for you."

Johnson, indeed, did many great things for Wake Forest during his five years (1977-81). He scored 1,749 points, more than any Deacon before him other than Dickie Hemric, Len Chappell, Brown, Griffin and Davis. He dished out 460 assists, second most in school history at the time he graduated. He was second-team All-ACC as a sophomore and junior and first-team as a senior in 1981. And as a freshman, he helped spark the Deacons' run all the way to the championship game of the Midwest Regional.

He wavered early in his career, becoming so homesick as a freshman that he considered transferring. But Tacy was unyielding, and refused to release him from his scholarship.

"I can't thank Coach Tacy enough for that," Johnson said later.

By staying, Johnson became one of the most popular players to ever wear a Wake Forest uniform. Though teammates called him "Hollywood" because of his flair for the dramatic, the fans called him "The Smiling Deacon" for his sunny countenance.

"Yeah, a lot of people think it's just showmanship," Johnson said during his playing days. "But it's genuine. It's my way of showing my love for the game, for being able to play basketball.

"What you are seeing here is one happy man."

A first-round pick of the Washington Bullets (the 11th pick overall) Johnson was named to the 1982 All-Rookie team. He played for the Bullets for seven years, for the Houston Rockets for one season, spent three seasons playing professional basketball in Italy, and then returned to the NBA in 1993 to play two seasons for the Phoenix Suns.

Upon retiring in 1994, he remained with the Suns in various capacities before being named head coach in 2001.

Johnson was inducted into the Wake Forest Hall of Fame in 1998.

Chapter 5
The Eighties

Frank Loses His Footing

To be Frank, he knew he would have to first get well. That was the sad conclusion Frank Johnson reached in the early weeks of the 1979-80 season, his first of two senior years.

Coming off a standout junior campaign, when he averaged 16.1 points and made second-team All-ACC, Johnson suffered a stress fracture in his foot while playing in a pickup game on campus in the fall of 1979.

"You know how it sounds when a finger snaps?" Johnson recalled. "It was like that, and I went down. I thought it was my ankle—I don't know why—and I tried to go to the training room. I couldn't get up."

Johnson tried to play, but after the sixth game of the season against Temple he realized his game wouldn't be the same until he recovered. He sat out the rest of the season, was granted a medical redshirt, and returned for his second senior season.

"I knew after that game that I wouldn't be able to play the way Frank Johnson wants to play," Johnson explained.

When Johnson went down, so did the Deacons. The sophomore-dominated team, left without an experienced backcourt leader, lost 11 of its final 18 games to finish 13-14 overall and 4-10 in the ACC.

Johnson's value to the program quickly became obvious the next season, when the Deacons won their first 14 games and shot up to the lofty ranking of No. 3 in the nation by mid-January. They finished the season at 22-7 and 9-5 in the ACC and reached the NCAA Tournament, where they lost to Boston College 67-64 in Tuscaloosa in the first round.

Johnson, that season, had never played better, averaging 16.2 points and 6.3 assists.

"Frank's sitting out a year was a blessing in disguise," Coach Carl Tacy said. "He had a chance to look at the entire league and think about his situation."

The season of observation may have paid dividends later, when Johnson became head coach of the Phoenix Suns. It certainly helped him make what had been a difficult transition from wing guard to point guard following the departure of Skip Brown.

"The good part is I spent a season actually watching basketball," Johnson said. "I guess all along I had the physical skills for the point. I didn't have the understanding, and that meant I didn't have the confidence.

"Seeing a game from the bench was a big change. I started to recognize why rhythm was so important, and how to control it. I saw how the game fits together, and what had to be done to get the most out of our players.

"A lot that Coach Tacy had told me over the years sort of fell into place in my mind. I was sure I could play the point even before the season began. I was confident again. I was glad."

Clearing Out Carmichael

At first glance, Wake Forest's 4-16 record at North Carolina's Carmichael Auditorium doesn't appear very impressive. In truth, the Deacons won more games there than any team besides North Carolina during the 20 seasons Carmichael served as the Tar Heels' home court.

From the time Carmichael opened against William & Mary on December 2, 1965 until North Carolina played its last game there against N.C. State on January 4, 1986, the Tar Heels enjoyed a home record of 169-20. Duke won the first game and last game it played at Carmichael, and lost all 18 in between. N.C. State, for all its success against North Carolina during the David Thompson glory days of the 1970s, was 3-18 in the arena. Virginia and Maryland were both 2-18 and Clemson was 0-20.

That's why so many people were so amazed on February 11, 1981, when the Deacons, to their utter glee, found themselves leading by 30 points in Carmichael Auditorium before cruising through the final minutes to an 84-68 victory.

Wake Forest, led by Johnson, Jim Johnstone, Alvis Rogers, Mike Helms and Guy Morgan, was a good team in 1981, good enough to peak at 20-2 before losing five of its final seven. But before the late-season fade, the Deacons provided their fans the memory of that magical moment in Carmichael, when they led 43-22 at half and then put the Tar Heels away by outscoring them 17-10 to start the second half.

While North Carolina struggled to score against Wake Forest's active zone defense, Helms hit 10 of 17 shots from the floor to lead the Deacons with 20 points.

"We could have gone out, sat on the points we had and waited for the game to end," Helms said. "But that was one of the things we didn't want to do. We wanted to keep scoring because the more points we put in, the harder they would have to work to catch up."

Coach Dean Smith of North Carolina absorbed the blame for the drubbing, saying he didn't have the Tar Heels, ranked No. 10 at the time, ready to play.

"I can't remember being dominated like that in I don't know how many years—especially here," Smith said. "We were embarrassed as a team."

Twenty years later, Tacy recalled the clogged aisles of Carmichael Auditorium as fans made their way to the exits.

"The stands were about half empty or half full, depending on how you want to look at it," Tacy said. "You could see them leaving, and I had never witnessed that before in that facility.

"They would stay to the end. But not that game."

Like many great stories, this one had an epilogue. The Deacons traveled to Chapel Hill a year later, with many of their fans expecting the worst, and knocked off the top-ranked Tar Heels 55-48. It was the first loss of the season for North Carolina, which would lose only once more (at Virginia) on the way to the NCAA title.

Wake Forest's other two victories in Carmichael were a stunning 91-90 upset over the seventh-ranked Tar Heels in 1970 and a 67-66 win over the fourth-ranked Tar Heels in 1977. Tacy, who coached the victories of 1977, 1981 and 1982, was the only opposing coach besides N.C. State's Norm Sloan to win three games in Carmichael Auditorium.

Too Strange Not to Be Real

Have you ever had one of those episodes in life that was strange, so serendipitous that you could almost hear the eerie music well up from some undetermined place?

In 1982, after hunting for golf clubs, former All-ACC guard Jackie Murdock of Wake Forest had an experience that was just too strange not to be real.

The salesman pitching Murdock a set of McGregor Hogan irons said there was something special about the one-iron.

"Somebody said it used to even belong to Hogan himself," the salesman said.

Murdock remembered distinctly a one-iron Hogan once had. So did most golf fans who knew anything about Hogan and his great comeback victory in the 1950 U.S. Open.

"I'd always admired Hogan, and remembered the bad bus wreck he was in in '49," Murdock said. "They thought he'd never play golf again. But he came back the next year and won the U.S. Open."

Needing a birdie to win, Hogan drove a one-iron onto the No. 18 green and dropped the putt for the victory. But the next time Hogan reached into his bag for the club, it had disappeared.

When Murdock's clubs arrived, he studied the one-iron closely. He took particular note of a well-worn spot about the size of a dime.

"It was just a perfectly round circle on the face of the club," Murdock said. "I began to wonder if there was something to (the salesman's comment)."

As fate would have it, golfer Lanny Wadkins, a star at Wake Forest before he became a standout on the PGA Tour, was inducted into the Wake Forest Sports Hall of Fame in 1982, the same year as Murdock. Murdock mentioned the club to Wadkins, who, again, as fate would have it, lived close to Hogan in Texas.

Wadkins carried he club back with him and showed it to Hogan. The club, Hogan said, was his long-lost one-iron.

"He sent me a little 'thank you' note for sending it to him," Murdock said.

Hogan donated the club to the collection of memorabilia at Golf House, headquarters for the U.S. Golf Association, which sanctions the U.S. Open.

"It was a miracle," Murdock said.

Derailed by Destiny

N.C. State's riveting run to the 1983 NCAA title ended, as many remember, in Albuquerque, New Mexico with Coach Jim Valvano dashing madly around the court following the Wolfpack's improbable victory over Houston. But there are Wake Forest fans who would just as soon forget how it began.

The Deacons faced N.C. State in the first round of the ACC Tournament in Atlanta. Wake Forest, which had been pounded by the Wolfpack 130-89 six days earlier in Raleigh, was 17-10. N.C. State, which had won four of six, was also 17-10. Both needed a win to bolster their shaky credentials for an invitation to the NCAA Tournament.

The game was tied at 70 with 4:15 remaining when Tacy directed the Deacons into a stall. Wake Forest ran the clock down to 30 seconds before calling time. With 20 seconds left, Rogers attempted a pass to Danny Young that was deflected by N.C. State's Sidney Lowe. Thurl Bailey came up with the prize, giving the Wolfpack the last shot.

Less than five seconds remained when forward Lorenzo Charles of the Wolfpack blew past Rogers on the way to the basket. Rogers was forced to foul Charles, who missed the first free throw but made the second for a 71-70 victory.

Still alive, the Wolfpack upended North Carolina and Virginia to win the ACC title and qualify for an automatic bid to the NCAA Tournament. Wake Forest, meanwhile, was relegated to the NIT, where it beat Murray State, Vanderbilt and South Carolina before losing to Fresno State 86-62 in the semifinals in New York's Madison Square Garden.

Toeing the sideline, Holmes threw the ball back over his shoulder just before he stepped out of bounds. Kenny Green of the Deacons intercepted the pass and passed to Delaney Rudd who launched a 25-foot jumper as the buzzer sounded. Rudd's bomb hit its target, forcing an overtime that the Deacons won when Young drove past Comegys for a layup and a 73-71 victory.

"He's a legend and we all respect what Coach Meyer has done," Rudd said after the game. "I know it's heartbreaking for them not being able to win the big one for him. But we've got a coach, and we've got a university and we want to build a tradition too."

Tacy had provided his own tournament subplot by stating that if Wake Forest were to win the national championship, he too would retire. Many thought that Tacy was just joking, but 20 years later he insisted that was not the case.

"I said it, and I would have done it," Tacy said. "It had been done before. Al McGuire was one to do it. It's a goal that you so badly want to achieve, and if you can do it, what's left?"

Wake Forest lost to Houston 68-63 in the Regional Final. The Deacons battled hard, and trailed only 57-55 with 5 1/2 minutes left. But ultimately they had no answer for Olajuwon, who made his first 13 shots from the floor and finished with 29 points, 12 rebounds and three blocked shots.

Good News

So what is a basketball coach to do with a skinny, undersized center with a jump shot as ugly as a Cruella DeVil on a bad hair day?

If said basketball coach is Tacy, then he puts him in the starting lineup and goes off and wins games.

Anthony Teachey, by all rights, was too much of a runt to excel at center in the game of power and muscle of ACC basketball. In 1983, Teachey's junior season, the list of ACC centers

Standing in Ray's Way

As battle cries go, "Retire Meyer" had both a r
reason for the Deacons to reach deep down
one of the memorable victories in school history.

By the time they had knocked off Kans:
Lincoln, Nebraska to advance to the regional sem
St. Louis, the Deacons had been painted as foils i
feel-good stories of the 1984 Tournament. The
DePaul, was coached by Ray Meyer, a legend;
Chicago basketball who had announced he woul
the season, his 42nd as the Demons' head coach.

Meyer's last DePaul team was one of his best,
sensus seemed to be that the Demons would b
Deacons to play Hakeem Olajuwon and the Hou
in the regional final.

But Wake Forest, which had lost three of its
regular-season games to finish 7-7 in the conferer
ideas. The Deacons felt overlooked by the media a
timent that dug ever deeper when a fan walking tl
the St. Louis Arena was overhead to wonder, "
Forest?'

"They keep calling it Lake Forest," Tacy obs
got to spell it out for them."

Assistant coach Mark Freidinger of the Dea
before the game that if Wake Forest could hang
pressure of the Demons trying to win one for
coach would prove oppressive. And indeed, afte
an eight-point lead with three minutes remaining
downs opened the door for a Deacons' comebac

Wake Forest had closed to 67-65 when Del
three critical turnovers—a backcourt violatio
McMillan, an errant alley-oop pass from Kenny
sailed over the head of Tyrone Corbin and an c
Dallas Comegys that forced teammate Kevin F
across the sideline to keep it from sailing into tl

included 7-4, 225-pound Ralph Sampson of Virginia, 6-11, 235-pound Brad Daugherty of North Carolina, 6-11, 215-pound Cozell McQueen of N.C. State and 6-10, 235-pound Yvon Joseph of Georgia Tech.

Teachey may have weighed 200 pounds before practice started. And, on tiptoes, he might have stood the 6-9 listed in the program. What was indisputable was that he shot one of the most unsightly jumpers in ACC history, a line drive released off his fingertips with an odd sideways spin.

For all his shortcomings, Teachey was as big a part of Wake Forest's success in 1983 and 1984 as anybody. He averaged 10.1 points and 8.5 rebounds for a 20-12 Deacon team in 1983, and as a senior averaged 13.1 points and 10 rebounds for a team that finished 23-9 and wasn't eliminated until a 68-63 loss to Hakeem Olajuwon and Houston in the final of the Midwest Regional.

To some folks back home in Goldsboro, Teachey was a guy who wasn't as good as he thought he was. He proved them wrong.

"Yeah, I heard them all," Teachey said. "They said I'd be back home looking for a job in less than a year, or I'd have to transfer to someplace else in order to play.

"Believe it or not, those people really helped me. I wanted to prove to them I could make it. I just kept telling myself that someday I would come back to Goldsboro, and those who did-n't believe in me were going to eat their words."

Teachey's smile was as beautiful as his shot was ugly. An ebullient person by nature, he was known as Anthony "Good News" Teachey during his career at Wake Forest. The tag came from the character Sheriff Roscoe in the popular television program *Dukes of Hazzard.* Episode after episode Sheriff Roscoe would run up to the Dukes' chief antagonist, Boss Hogg, shouting "Good news, good news."

Making His Father Happy

A couple of weeks after he signed to play basketball for Wake Forest, in 1983, Mark Cline played for an All-Star team from West Virginia that was taking on an AAU team from the Soviet Union.

That was the night Cline realized just how unpopular his decision had been.

"I got more boos than the Russians," Cline explained.

A great deal of effort and energy had been expended in keeping Cline, a product of Williamson, West Virginia, home to play his college basketball for West Virginia University. A two-time West Virginia Player of the Year, he was wined and dined on more than one occasion by Jay Rockefeller, then governor of the state, on behalf of the Mountaineers.

"It was pretty high-powered to keep me in the state," Cline said.

Wake Forest and West Virginia weren't the only two schools in hot pursuit of Cline. After receiving 2,000 letters from 168 programs, Cline narrowed his choice to Wake Forest, Kentucky, West Virginia and Clemson.

Ultimately blood proved thicker than the folder of letters he had received. His father, Herb Cline, had been one of Wake Forest's most accomplished athletes of the pre-ACC years, a star receiver in football and standout center in basketball.

In football, he set a Wake Forest record with three touchdown catches in one game. In basketball he was All-Southern Conference three years and co-captain in 1942, the year he won the Royster Medal for the top academic record among athletes.

Herb Cline had sent his son to Wake Forest's basketball camp when Mark was eight, even though the minimum age was said to be 10 years old. Though the father left the decision up to the son, the son was determined to make his old man happy when he signed with Wake Forest.

"I think that may have been my main reason," Mark said. "He's done so much for me, and I'd like to make him happy. This is where I wanted to be. I knew that after I evaluated it, and I think it was probably because of him."

Mark Cline ended up scoring 1,202 points for Wake Forest from 1984 through 1987, and was one of the few ACC-caliber athletes on teams that suffered losing seasons his junior and senior years. But his problems began even before Tacy unexpectedly resigned following his sophomore season, to be replaced by Bob Staak.

As a freshman, Cline suffered a dislocated thumb and contracted mononucleosis. He sat the bench, for the first time of his life. His girlfriend broke up with him.

He was so miserable he contemplated leaving Wake Forest.

"When I left Williamson, I thought I had about 5,000 friends," Cline said. "When I returned, I found out I had about three. I was shocked.

"Everywhere I went everyone kept saying, 'You made a mistake. You should have gone to WVU.' I couldn't believe it. I had never faced adversity. I didn't know how to handle it.

"I was thinking about leaving school. I was thinking about a thousand different things. Finally, I decided to sit down and think everything through. When I finished, I decided to go back down there and give it my best shot."

Though the NBA career many had predicted for him never materialized, Cline found his post-college niche in coaching. When Wake Forest played Virginia Commonwealth in the first round of the 2004 NCAA Regional in Raleigh, Cline was on the VCU staff of head coach Jeff Capel.

Short and To the Point

Tacy sat behind his desk in the basketball office of Wake Forest. On the other side of the desk sat three recruits, all guards.

One was Tommy Amaker, a 6-0 high school senior from Falls Church, Virginia. Another was Keith Gatlin, a 6-5 high school senior from Grimesland, N.C. The third was Tyrone Bogues, a 5-3 high school senior from Baltimore, Maryland.

"I have one scholarship available," Tacy told them. "The first one who accepts it, gets it."

Amaker, later to become head coach at Seton Hall and Michigan, turned down Wake Forest to play at Duke. Gatlin opted to play for Lefty Driesell at Maryland.

That left Bogues, who unlike Amaker and Gatlin, had precious few other options. He signed with Wake Forest.

"You know the old story—we thought he was somebody's brother," teammate Rudd said. "The first time we noticed him was in the gym on his first visit to Wake Forest. He was so short he couldn't have been a recruit. It was hard to believe."

After Bogues's freshmen season of 1984, it appeared the Deacons, by signing the shortest player in ACC history, got the short end of the stick. Amaker, playing 36 minutes a game, averaged 7.5 points and ranked fifth in the ACC with 4.8 assists per game. Gatlin, playing 24 minutes a game, averaged 6.2 points.

Bogues, playing only 10 minutes a game, scored 37 points all season, for an average of 1.2.

But if anyone has ever proven that first impressions can be misleading, Bogues is the man. Battling his way into the starting lineup after Danny Young graduated, Bogues, as it turned out, led the ACC in assists and steals his final three seasons.

"I wouldn't have believed it if I hadn't seen it," Rudd said. "After his freshman year I knew he'd be a great player."

The records will also show that Bogues was playing in the NBA long after Amaker and Gatlin were done.

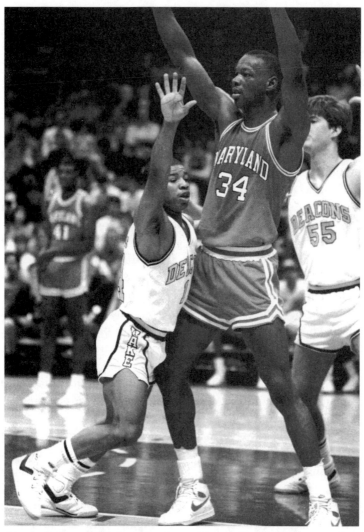

Tyrone Bogues didn't have height on his side, but he had more than enough heart and talent to make up for it. (Courtesy of Wake Forest Media Relations)

A Threat of Death

There's an old country saying that it's not the size of the dog in the fight that matters, but rather the size of the fight in the dog.

By that measure, Bogues proved on January 17, 1985 that inside his undersized 5-3, 135-pound body was a huge heart.

It was a skeleton Wake Forest team that played at Duke that night. Senior Chuck Kepley was recovering from arthroscopic knee surgery and freshman Jeff McGill had just announced he was transferring from Wake Forest, leaving Tacy only nine available players.

Nine, on this night, was enough. Bogues, despite giving up 11 inches, was all over junior Johnny Dawkins, holding the Blue Devil star to four field goals on 16 attempts for eight points. Bogues, meanwhile, contributed 12 points, seven assists and four steals, and hit the clinching free throws with nine seconds remaining in the Deacons' 91-89 overtime victory.

"I thought Bogues was just tremendous," Tacy said. "I don't know how long he's going to have to play like this before he gets the recognition he deserves. We certainly know what he means to our team."

Only later would it be revealed just how much courage Bogues had shown that night. Unbeknownst to the general public, Bogues played under the threat of death.

A stranger to Bogues from nearby Clemmons named Warren Brooks, incensed at ABC Administrator Lewis Cutright, had told the secretary of the Winston-Salem Board of Alderman that Bogues would be killed if Cutright were not fired.

A chilling transcript from the phone conversation read: "Make sure Tyrone Bogues doesn't play Thursday or Friday night. On Friday morning if the aldermen go to the morgue they will see Tyrone stretched out there."

Bogues traveled to Durham in a separate car from his teammates, and security at Cameron Indoor Stadium was tight.

Five months later, on June 27, 1985, a Forsyth County Superior Judge sentenced Brooks to three years for his threat on Bogues's life.

Heroes of a Lost Season

In 1988, a disastrous season by most objective standards, two small Wake Forest guards proved just what can be achieved by a good college try.

By the late stretches of the 10-18 campaign, after injuries had cost Staak the services of Robert Siler, Daric Keys, Tony Black and Todd Sanders, the Deacons were down to six scholarship players. The list did not include Steve Ray, a walk-on who was pressed into extensive action at point guard.

In a late-season double-overtime 69-67 home loss to Virginia, Ray acquitted himself by playing 33 minutes without a turnover. He scored four points to go with three rebounds and an assist.

But one of the six available scholarship players who gave Staak everything he could have asked for was Cal Boyd, a 6-0 junior from Smyrna, Georgia, who averaged 11.3 points.

One of the most accurate long-range shooters in Wake Forest history, Boyd, through the 2004 season, held the school record with a career three-point accuracy of 47 percent. In 1989, Boyd shot 50 percent from beyond the arc—a season record at Wake Forest until broken by Ricardo Peral's 51 percent in 1996—and was named the team's most valuable player.

In the lost season of 1988, Boyd provided one of the few moments worth remembering when his 18 points sparked the Deacons to a stunning 83-30 victory over North Carolina in Greensboro. The Deacons were 6-9 at the time, having lost to such undistinguished opponents as Siena, Furman and Coastal Carolina. The Tar Heels were 14-2 and ranked No. 3 in the nation.

Down 14 in the second half, the Deacons caught fire and burned North Carolina for their first victory over the Tar Heels since 1982.

Boyd, to his credit, was dealing with far more than his lack of size and quickness. His father was suffering from leukemia, and a brain hemorrhage had cost him his sight. His mother had been overcome with a severe depression resulting from her husband's condition and a reaction to blood pressure medication.

Boyd's profile in courage that season was another example of how little fans and media often know of what many college athletes are privately going through. In a feature story in the *Winston-Salem Journal* published January 28, the day of the North Carolina upset, Boyd adamantly refused to portray himself as a victim.

"I don't want this to come off as: Everybody should feel sorry for Cal Boyd, because I'm certainly not feeling sorry for myself," he said. "You just have to go on with life."

"We All Just Only Wish"

Every school has its "If Only" stories. Many chronicle the talented player who, because of injury or personal fallibility, never realizes his potential.

At Wake Forest, people will long wonder just how good Robert Siler could have been—"If Only" he had remained healthy.

Recruited from Siler City before the 1988 season, during the depths of the Staak era, Siler was stunning athlete. Quick, strong and explosive, the 6-3, 200-pound Siler had been a Parade All-America tailback who scored 37 touchdowns in his senior season at Jordan-Matthews High School. During his spare time, he set the school's triple-jump record.

Playing the ninth game of his freshman season at Wake Forest, against American University, Siler went up for a short jumper, felt his knee twist and heard his knee ligament pop. He returned after surgery and extensive rehabilitation, only to suffer another torn ligament in 1990.

Siler, as it turned out, played 94 games at Wake Forest, averaging 9.7 points for his career. But from the time he was hurt as a freshman, every game he played later reminded those in attendance just what might have been.

"We all just only wish we could have seen a healthy Robert Siler for four years and seen what he could have become," Coach Dave Odom said.

The Play That Never Works

The record book shows that Staak coached 114 games at Wake Forest. In the interest of accuracy, Staak should probably be credited with 114 1/2 games. In his last regular-season game with the Deacons, a four-overtime marathon against N.C. State, Staak worked time and a half.

The Deacons, stumbling home to a seventh-place ACC finish, summoned up one more valiant effort against the Wolfpack in Greensboro on March 4, 1989. Wake Forest would be eliminated from the ACC Tournament by Duke six days later to close at 13-15 overall and 3-11 in conference play. N.C. State, in Jim Valvano's next to last season, won 22 and lost nine and finished first in the ACC regular season at 10-4.

But with two seconds remaining on the Greensboro Coliseum scoreboard, the Deacons led by three points and had the upset in hand. Or so they thought.

Guard Kelsey Weems of the Wolfpack made the first of two free throws, then intentionally missed the second. Teammate Rodney Monroe, the leading scorer in N.C. State history, grabbed the rebound and launched a high arching fadeaway jump shot that slipped through the net as the buzzer sounded.

Overtime.

"I was just hoping," guard Chris Corchiani of N.C. State said. "I've seen that situation before, but the play never works. A guy makes the second free throw or misses the rim. This time, it worked. Rodney hit the miracle shot."

The Deacons were crestfallen.

"I was standing under the goal and watching the ball hit the net," forward Chris King of Wake Forest said. "I said to myself, 'I can't believe this.' The coach told us to block out and we didn't."

Wake Forest had three more cracks at the upset, but failed to score on the final possession of the first three overtimes. Staak, for reasons of his own, never called time to set up the final play. The Wolfpack finally got enough leverage in the fourth overtime to hold on for a 110-103 victory.

"I've never seen a game like that, not even on TV," Corchiani said. "It's one of the great games you could ever be involved in. Every play was big, and every player hustled. Before every overtime, somebody on the bench would say, 'One more overtime, one more overtime.' We wanted to win.

"When we got tired out there, Coach V grabbed us and told us to hold on. He said we should win this one because it's one of the greatest ACC games ever, and what a wonderful feeling it would be."

For Wake Forest, the final score was not a pretty sight. Neither was the scene at midcourt following the final buzzer. Staak turned on a heckler in the Deacons' student section and yelled at the antagonist for a couple of minutes before making his way to the home locker room.

"I'm as drained as I think I've ever been after a game," Staak said in the press conference. "Imagine what the players must feel like. They played their hearts out."

The game, which began shortly after 4 p.m. and ended at 6:57, set a standard for longest conference game in ACC history. Only N.C. State (against Canisius in the 1956 NCAA

Tournament) and North Carolina (against Tulane in 1976) had ever before played four overtimes.

Forward Chucky Brown of the Wolfpack played 59 minutes and scored a career-high 34 points.

But instead of being allowed to absorb what they had just witnessed, the fans at Greensboro Coliseum were rushed to the exits by the public address announcer. The championship game of the MEAC Tournament was scheduled to begin later on the same floor.

And ESPN was in town to televise it.

Virginia's Loss, Wake Forest's Gain

By the 1989 season, it became apparent to Coach Terry Holland of Virginia that his assistant, Odom, was destined to be a head coach in the ACC. The only question was where.

Wake Forest was in need of a coach after the 1989 season, and had requested an interview with Odom. But Holland had already planned to retire after the 1990 season.

So Holland approached Jim Copeland, the director of athletics at Virginia, with the proposal that would keep Odom in Charlottesville. Holland suggested that Copeland assure Odom he would become head coach after Holland stepped down.

"And he said, 'No, I can't guarantee Dave the job—I can only guarantee him he'll be a candidate,'" Holland related. "I came back to Dave and said, 'You don't have any choice but to go to Wake Forest.'"

There are those in Charlottesville who will always regret the one who got away. Odom coached at Wake Forest for 12 seasons, winning 240 games and directing the Deacons to eight appearances in the NCAA Tournament and three appearances in the NIT. Jeff Jones, Holland's successor at Virginia, coached the Cavaliers eight seasons, winning 146 games and directing Virginia to five appearances in the NCAA and one in the NIT.

Chapter 6
The Nineties

Territorial Rights

Jerry Steele, a forward for Wake Forest from 1959 through 1961, was in his first season as the head coach at Guilford College when he noticed that he didn't have a point guard—which is not unlike a baseball coach realizing he doesn't have a catcher or a football coach in desperate need of a quarterback.

But he did notice a defensive back from the football team who handled himself pretty well on the basketball court in intramural play. And he noticed that despite the student's lack of size, at best 5-10, he had huge, oversized hands that allowed him to handle the ball with the aplomb of a much bigger player.

So Steele drafted the player to play point guard for Guilford. The student's name was Dave Odom, who almost 30 years later would become Wake Forest's head basketball coach.

"I had territorial rights," Steele said later. "We needed a guard who could handle the ball and run the show. And he did it much better than I anticipated anyone could, especially someone who had been away from it a year or so.

"He made all four players better, and he was content to do that. I guess the term is leadership."

The bond between the coach and his point guard was strengthened one night when Guilford was in Newberry, S.C. to play a game. Steele received a call saying that Odom's father, William, had died back home in Goldsboro, N.C.

Odom, when told, insisted on playing the game. He also asked that Steele not tell any of his teammates.

"He went out and played, and after the game we hit the road for Goldsboro," Steele recalled.

"If You Can Play, You Can Play"

After the dark days of the mid-to-late 1980s, when Wake Forest suffered five straight losing seasons, those who live and die with the fortunes of the Deacon basketball team thought they could see a crack of light late in the winter of 1990. Coach Dave Odom's first team at Wake Forest, having lost its first 11 conference games, beat Maryland, Virginia and N.C. State in succession.

Even more impressive was the fact the wins against Virginia and N.C. State came on the road.

Hopes soared considerably the next fall when two heralded freshmen, Rodney Rogers and Randolph Childress led the Deacons to an 86-84 exhibition victory over the German National Team. The quality of the opponent wasn't as impressive as the way the Deacons won. Rogers and Childress scored 13 of Wake Forest's final 17 points and Rogers made a driving basket to win the game.

After Childress finished with 23 points and Rogers piled up 19 points and 10 rebounds, Odom predicted more to come.

"If you can play, you can play," Odom said. "And I think they can."

Even with Rogers averaging 16.3 points and 7.9 rebounds as a freshman, and Childress adding 14 points a game, the Deacons jeopardized their chances of making the NCAA Tournament by falling to 15-9 in mid-February with losses at North Carolina and Maryland. The trip to College Park was particularly painful, when the Deacons lost 86-78 to a Terrapins team that would finish seventh in the ACC at 5-9.

But if there was one game that got the Deacons back over the hump, it followed the very next day back in Winston-Salem. Playing host to a weak Clemson team, the Deacons rolled to a cathartic 81-55 victory.

Rogers proved too much for the Tigers when he amassed 23 points, eight rebounds, six steals and four assists.

"I don't know if I've ever been associated with a team that I am prouder of than I am of this team today," Odom said afterward.

The victory set in motion a three-game winning streak that assured Wake Forest its first trip to the NCAA Tournament since 1984. The Deacons beat Louisiana Tech 71-65 in Atlanta, then lost two days later to Alabama 96-88.

They would be invited to the NCAA Tournament six more seasons in a row before being relegated to the NIT in 1998.

Surviving the Street

If Rogers's inner strength had weakened, he would have never made it out of McDougald Terrace, his combat-zone of a neighborhood in a less-than-ritzy section of Durham. But Rogers, a man-child as a young teenager, remained as strong as he would need to be.

Rogers's father, Willie Wadsworth, died when Rodney was seven. His brother, Stanley, served time for armed robbery. His mother, Estelle Spencer, almost died in an automobile crash

The fact that Rodney Rogers thrived as a Demon Deacon wasn't surprising given everything Rogers had to overcome as a teenager on the mean streets of Durham. (Courtesy of Wake Forest Media Relations)

when Rodney was a sophomore at Durham Hillside High School.

But there were good people in Durham who wouldn't let Rogers down. And even some of the not-so-good people, the drug dealers who hawked their wares on the street corners of McDougald Terrace, could see enough promise in the strapping young Rogers that they left him alone.

"It's just something you've got to be strong enough to say 'I'm not going to mess with it,'" Rogers said. "You've got to have priorities. You've got to know what you want to do in life.

"You see other guys who were right there at the time, and one little mistake and they blew it. So you say to yourself, 'If I ever get to that point, I'm never going to blow it.'"

With his mother convalescing, Rogers was informally adopted by a masonry contractor named Nathaniel Brooks and his wife Barbara. Instead of living alone in McDougald Terrace, Rogers lived with the Brooks' family during his final years of high school.

Nathaniel Brooks told Rogers right off he must abide by one rule. He would be treated exactly like the two sons of the family, Daryl and Nathaniel Jr.

"That was understood," Brooks said. "He looked to me as a father image. If he has any questions or problems, he knows he can discuss them with me and my wife.

"We don't try to take the place of his mother, but we offer him spiritual and personal guidance. When he comes and stays with us, we go to church."

By 1991, Rogers was the ACC Rookie of the Year. By 1992, he was first-team All-ACC. By 1993, he was the ACC Player of the Year. By the summer of 1993, he was the first-round pick of the NBA's Denver Nuggets.

And by the spring of 2004, he was finishing his 11th season in the NBA.

The Gift of Gab

In his 12 seasons as Wake Forest's head basketball coach, Odom proved adept in many pursuits, as his 240-132 record indicates. He recruited well enough to land the likes of Rogers, Childress, Tim Duncan and Josh Howard. He knew how to beat Duke, as he did a remarkable nine straight times from February 13 1993 until February 5, 1997. And few coaches coached tenacious half-court defense any better.

But what Odom has always done best is talk. Man how the man can talk.

Inheriting the gift of gab from father William, a one-time mechanic who would keep climbing the business ladder until he owned the Pontiac-Cadillac dealership in Wilson, N.C., Odom was a favorite of the media during an era of dwindling accessibility to players and coaches. His detailed, vivid and often soul-searching postgame recaps, which would begin behind the podium in the media room and end much, much later in the corner of the Wake Forest locker room, were legendary. A favorite Odom technique—just to keep the conversation flowing—was the rhetorical question.

"Did we show poise in the final minutes? Maybe not. Did we crack and fall completely apart? I don't believe so. Whose fault was it that we didn't win? I'll have to take the blame for that."

The weekly ACC teleconference supposedly limits each coach to 10 minutes. Odom routinely talked twice that long. His wife, Lynn, would chide him about his radio talk show because, due to the length of his answers, so few callers got to ask questions.

The Atlantic Coast Conference once held a media conference in downtown New York to promote a tournament. The featured speakers were Commissioner Gene Corrigan, Coach Pat Kennedy of Florida State and Odom. When Odom's time came to stand behind the podium, he talked, and talked and talked.

Odom was still talking, as the story went (on and on) when Corrigan and Kennedy walked over, lifted him by his elbows, and carried him away from the microphones.

Jerry Wainwright, a former assistant under Odom who became head coach at UNC Wilmington and Richmond, said he knew how to brace for Odom's verbal siege.

"When he started talking, I would make sure I always stocked up on extra dessert," Wainwright said. "I told him once before he began talking at a postseason banquet to make sure he finished before the next season began."

Providing the Solid Foundation

Wake Forest announced a media conference for April 26, 1993, at Joel Coliseum, at which time Rogers would reveal whether he intended to return to Wake Forest for his senior season or make himself available for the NBA draft.

Coliseum workers spent the morning setting up a meeting room, complete with microphones, rows of chairs and a black curtain to serve as backdrop. Perhaps it was a portent of things to come when the door was opened to the room and the curtain, catching the breeze, toppled over.

Sandbags were brought in to prop up the hollow poles holding the curtain. In the media conference to come, those in attendance learned that Odom would need to do some propping up of his own after Rogers announced he would leave Wake Forest for the NBA.

Rogers said he was making the move for his mother, who had been scarred in a bad automobile wreck five years earlier in Durham.

"You have to look at my mom, her situation and all the trouble she's been through and all the adversity I've had," Rogers told the assembled media. "It's just a way to pay her back, a woman who would give me her last dime just so I would be happy. Now I want to see her happy."

For Rogers the heavy lifting was done the day he walked into Odom's office and told him he was leaving for the NBA. First he talked with assistants Wainwright, Ricky Stokes and Larry Davis.

"The coaches were saying, 'You've got to be a man and go tell him,'" Rogers said. "I just had to keep my foot down and go in and talk to him. And whether he liked it or not, he couldn't change my mind.

"I didn't know how he would react to it. I didn't know if he would get angry or anything. But he surprised me. He was really helpful and he said 'If this is what you want to do, OK.' He said, 'Let's talk about the people you want to bring in.'"

When Rogers left, he left with Odom's blessings. At the media conference, Odom heaped praise on his departing star.

"I think what he has given us is more of a solid foundation to build on," Odom said. "We'll take that and we'll go on, and we'll continue to do very well."

Odom was right. The next season, 1994, the Deacons won 21 and lost 12, finished third in the ACC with a 9-7 record and received their fourth straight invitation to the NCAA Tournament.

From One Stage to Another

Maybe he just knew how to act the part, but few players in Wake Forest history ever got more out of their abilities than Marc Blucas. A 6-3 guard from Girard, Pennsylvania who played from 1991 through 1994, Blucas, by most estimations, was too short and slow to guard a player as talented as Duke's Grant Hill. But he would anyway, and do so in surprisingly effective fashion.

Marc Blucas was considered too short and too slow to keep pace with the ACC's elite guards—but scouts overlooked one intangible: The kid had passion. (Courtesy of Wake Forest Media Relations)

Blucas eventually made his mark not in basketball but in acting, displaying the same confidence and determination he showed on the court to carve an impressive career in television and film. But there were signs during his playing days that he could certainly emote.

One such memorable occasion was the angry aftermath of the opening game of the 1994 season. The Deacons were playing in the Great Alaska Shootout in Anchorage and had just been upended 70-68 by Alaska-Anchorage of the NCAA's Division II.

The walls of Anchorage's Sullivan Arena were thin, far too thin to prevent the media assembled outside the Deacons' locker room from hearing Blucas's blistering R-rated tirade at his teammates. A senior who would assume a mantel of leadership, Blucas took the loss personally, as he let his teammates know in rather graphic terms.

Wake Forest rebounded to beat Hawaii and Wisconsin-Green Bay and return from Alaska 2-1. The Deacons won 21 and lost 12 in 1994 and Blucas averaged 6.4 points and 3.4 rebounds while shooting 47 percent from the floor and 48 percent from 3-point range.

As rough and tumble as he needed to be, Blucas also led the Deacons with 96 fouls and fouled out of seven games.

"I'm Getting Hot"

In the third game of his college career, with the Deacons embroiled in a close game at sixth-ranked Alabama, Childress shot an airball. Moments later he took another shot. Again, nothing but air.

That's when Odom, in his second season as Wake Forest's head coach, learned all he would need to know about Randolph Childress.

"Don't take me out now," Childress implored, as he ran by the Wake Forest bench. "I'm getting hot."

The Deacons lost 96-95 in overtime, but Childress, true to his word, made seven of 12 field goal attempts to score 22 points.

Childress, Odom liked to say, was fearless, so much so that he could miss 10 straight shots, as he did at Vanderbilt on December 8, 1993, and then make two three-pointers in the final minute of the second half to send the game into overtime.

"I don't care if I make 10 shots in a row or miss 10 shots in a row," Childress once said. "The next shot I take is the only one that counts."

In 1990, the year before Childress arrived, the Deacons finished 3-11 in the ACC. In 1992, the year he missed while recuperating from knee surgery, they finished 7-9 in the conference. In the four years Childress played for Wake Forest, the Deacons were 39-23 in conference play. In 1995, with Childress scoring a record 107 points in the ACC Tournament, the Deacons beat Duke, Virginia and North Carolina for their first ACC title in 33 years.

"He had what we needed at the time that he came here," Odom said. "We needed confidence. Because if you think back, Wake was a talented team that couldn't finish it.

"We'd get right to the door and couldn't open it. And he was one of those who didn't ask why. He asked why not. His attitude just permeated the whole team and really the whole campus."

Opposing fans hated Childress with a passion. They had their reasons.

"I can't imagine anybody having more confidence in me than I have in myself," Childress said. "If I could, that wouldn't say very much for me."

And there were times when Odom had trouble stomaching his star guard as well. Odom and Childress shared one of the ACC's classic love-hate relationships. In the heat of battle,

Odom would bark at Childress. Childress, never shy, would bark right back.

But Childress was always mindful to show respect for Odom to the media and public.

"My relationship with Coach, it's funny," Childress said. "He's a very emotional coach, and I'm a very emotional player.

"How many coaches tell you, 'It's O.K. for us to argue and disagree?' None that I know of. If I had gone somewhere like North Carolina, and I disagreed with a Dean Smith, he would throw me so far down at the end of the bench that I wouldn't even think about playing."

Bedeviling Duke

In athletics, it's funny how sometimes one team simply seems to have another team's number. So when the number of Wake Forest's consecutive victories over Duke reached nine in the early to mid-90s, the streak couldn't help but do a number on the Blue Devils' heads.

Other than the back-to-back ACC titles in 1995 and 1996 and 12 straight appearances in postseason play, the nine straight wins over Duke was probably the high-water mark of Odom's 12 years at Wake Forest. What made the accomplishment so impressive was that, other than 1995, when poor health and the strain of his profession forced Coach Mike Krzyzewski to the sidelines and the Blue Devils finished 13-18, the Deacons were almost always beating a Duke team ranked among college basketball's best.

The streak began with a 98-86 victory at Duke on February 13, 1993, when the Blue Devils were ranked No. 3 coming off their second consecutive national championship. The last victory of the streak was an 81-69 win at Duke on January 11, 1997, when the Blue Devils were ranked No. 10.

In the other seven victories, the Blue Devils were ranked No. 2 twice, No. 10 once, No. 11 once, No. 19 once and unranked three times.

Five of the victories, interestingly enough, came at Cameron Indoor Stadium, considered one of the most intimidating home courts in college basketball. The Deacons won three straight in Joel Coliseum and one in Greensboro in the first round of the 1995 ACC Tournament.

Rogers, returning home to Durham for his final game against Duke, made 14 of 16 shots from the floor to score a career-high 35 points in Cameron Indoor Stadium in 1993 in the first victory of the streak. A year later, freshman Tim Duncan warned of things to come when he piled up 14 points and eight rebounds against the second-ranked Blue Devils in a 78-69 victory in Joel Coliseum.

But Childress was the player most associated with Wake Forest's dominance over Duke, and rightfully so. In six games during the streak, Childress hit 44 of 86 shots from the floor (51 percent), averaged 25.5 points a game and in back-to-back seasons hit the winning bucket to beat the Blue Devils in Cameron Indoor Stadium.

Odom invariably winced when asked to explain the Deacons' mastery of the Blue Devils. He loathed talking about it, at least in public, knowing the more he said the more he would inspire Krzyzewski and his Blue Devils to do something about it.

But he did offer one explanation after the third of the nine straight wins, the 78-69 home victory in 1994.

"I think it's style," Odom said. "Our kids attack. Duke's kids attack. It's style. When both teams attack, you've got a chance. Play gets loose."

Blucas, a senior in 1994 who had his hand in the first three victories, said it was simply a matter of the Deacons refusing to be intimidated by reputation.

"We prepare in a way that they're not this colossal team that no one can beat," Blucas explained. "Just because they have those four letters across their chest, other teams get scared of that.

"I think a lot of teams fall prey to that tradition of Duke, and we don't do that."

Randolph Steps Up By Stepping Back

To say that Cameron Indoor Stadium was going crazy wouldn't be completely accurate.

After all, Wake Forest was in the house, and whenever Duke is playing a heated ACC rival the famous arena pretty much stays crazy all the time.

So the customary cacophony rocked Cameron as the final seconds were ticking down on the Deacons' visit to second-ranked Duke on January 13, 1994. Wake Forest, which had trailed by seven with five minutes remaining, had cut the lead to 68-66 with less than 15 seconds left. Childress squared up on Duke's Hill right of the foul line.

Faking as though he were heading into the lane, Childress instead stepped back behind the three-point line. Hill, momentarily off balance, lunged at the ball coming off Childress's fingers.

The ball cleared Hill's fingertips, sailed through the air and swished through the nets with 11 seconds remaining.

The scoreboard didn't register the basket.

Standing before his bench, Krzyzewski thought the shot had been launched from inside the three-point arc, which would have only tied the game at 68. So when Hill missed a jumper from the key as the buzzer sounded, Krzyzewski prepared for overtime.

Only then was he informed by the officials that the game was over, and he had lost.

"I was shocked that the game was over—I'll be honest with you," Krzyzewski said. "That shouldn't be. That was a mistake on my part, but I don't think the score ever went up."

Childress said he knew what he was doing.

"I was very conscious of it being a three," Childress said. "Because I didn't want to go into overtime."

One Seriously Troubling Thought

Pete Gaudet is a kind man and sympathetic figure to those who followed ACC basketball during the 1990s. He was the good solider who shouldered the load as interim Duke coach in 1995 after Krzyzewski, wracked with back pain, stepped aside 12 games into the season.

The Blue Devils finished 13-18 overall and last in the ACC with a 2-14 conference mark. Shortly thereafter Gaudet was gone, not to be retained by Krzyzewski.

One lasting memory of Gaudet is from the late afternoon hours of February 11, 1995. Earlier that day, his Blue Devils, playing one of their best games under his stewardship, had led 11th-ranked Wake Forest with less than a minute to go in Cameron Indoor Stadium, only to lose 62-61.

Pacing the halls of the arena, Gaudet happened upon the media room where a couple of sportswriters were just finishing their stories. The men exchanged pleasantries and the sportswriters expressed their condolences on the tough loss.

Gaudet, in tired, drained tones, talked about how excited center Eric Meeks had been when he dunked off a fast break for a 61-60 lead with 30 seconds to go.

Then Meeks, as he later confided to Gaudet, had one seriously troubling thought.

The thought?

"Childress," Gaudet said.

Childress, the Deacons' senior guard, was on a lot of minds at Cameron Indoor Stadium that day. For the second straight year, Childress beat the Blue Devils with a game-winning shot. The year before he had knocked in a three-pointer over Hill for the win. This time, he drained a 12-footer with six seconds to go to put the Deacons ahead 62-61, and Wake Forest survived a miss by Jeff Capel at the buzzer.

But Childress wasn't through tormenting his Duke rivals. First he took out his gum and whipped it into the taunting Duke student section. Then he picked up the ball near mid-court, took his windup and hurled the ball over the backboard at one end of the arena.

The ball soared through the air until it smacked into the face of an unsuspecting fan still sitting in his upper-deck seat.

As Childress was realizing what he had done, sophomore Duncan stood beside him, critiquing Childress's form.

"Decent arm," Duncan deadpanned. "Nice follow through."

The enraged Duke fans, seeing nothing nice about Childress, rained debris all down on Childress as he attempted to finish an on-court television interview. Later Childress expressed his regret for having hit the fan with the ball, but couldn't resist taking one last shot at the Cameron Crazies.

"I apologize to the fan for doing that," Childress said. "At the same time I'm not going to sit here and let everyone make it seem like I'm the bad guy. Their guys throwing ice and hitting our guys, is a lot worse.

"After the game I had to get a police escort to do an interview. That's ridiculous. I'm really sorry to the lady or man I hit. But to the crowd, I'm not one that cares for the crowd, anyway."

"His Will Overcomes Everything"

The greatest gift Childress got for Christmas as a nine-year old was a lesson he will never forget.

The form of the lesson: A video game that his stepfather, Reggie Boggs, had been secretly slipping out of its box and playing while Randolph was away at school.

The essence of the lesson: If you quit, you lose.

"By the time Christmas came I was pretty good, and Randolph had never played it," Boggs said. "So I was beating him pretty bad, and he was crying and wanting to quit, but I wouldn't let him quit. I gave him the book and told him to learn how to play it.

"About two days later he started beating me, and I think I've beaten him maybe one time since."

So even at nine years old, Childress displayed a burning will to win that would manifest itself time and again during his five years at Wake Forest.

"He's a player who gives his all all the time," his coach, Odom, noted. "When he wins he can see an even higher plateau that can be reached. In a loss, though the setback is obvious, to him it's just a temporary thing. It's just something that we've got to overcome. But it will be done.

"In his life, nothing is ever permanent—except his will. His will is always there. His will overcomes everything."

"As Best I Can Remember"

Cocky to the point of arrogant, Childress gave opponents sufficient reason to dislike him. But the media covering the ACC loved Childress, for two good reasons. He insisted on taking the shot that decided a game, and make or miss, he never minded talking about it later.

In a day of cluster television coverage, when newspaper reporters began to find more and more players and coaches to be more and more uncooperative, Childress was always available. He'd talk after scoring 25 points in a victory. He'd talk after scoring four points in a loss. Like his coach, Odom, Childress always loved to talk.

A classic case in point was Wake Forest's game at Maryland in 1994, Childress's junior season. Playing not far from his hometown of Clinton, Maryland, Childress suffered through an abysmal game. He made only one of eight shots from the floor, missed all five of his three-point attempts and finished with four points.

With the clock mercifully running down on Maryland's 81-58 drubbing, Duncan rebounded a missed shot, wheeled around and inadvertently whacked his elbow across Childress's nose. Childress left the game, not to return.

Assigned to cover the game for the *Winston-Salem Journal,* I was waiting to enter the Wake Forest locker room when John Justus, the Deacons' Sports Information Director, walked over.

"I just wanted to warn you that Randolph is pretty out of it," Justus said. "They think he might have a broken nose."

"Does that mean I shouldn't talk to him?" I asked.

"Oh, no, you can talk to him," Justus said. "I just wanted to let you know he might not make a whole lot of sense."

Upon admittance to the locker room, I spied Childress sitting in front of his locker staring down at the floor. I pulled up a nearby chair and sat down, so he wouldn't have to lift his head.

His nose, it would be determined the next day, had indeed been broken.

"So what happened, Randolph?" I asked, my head inches from his.

"As best I can remember," Randolph said, beginning a characteristically candid, if somewhat scattered, account of one of the worst nights of his young life.

As a reporter who has seen players with hangnails hide in the training room, I haven't forgotten that night. And I intend not to.

Randolph's World

It's important to remember that even before the ACC Tournament of 1995, Childress was already one of Wake Forest's all-time heroes. His jersey No. 22 had been retired in an emotional ceremony at the last regular-season game against N.C. State, the day he scored 21 points in an 83-68 victory and passed Skip Brown to become the Deacons' third all-time leading scorer behind Dickie Hemric and Len Chappell.

But leave it to Childress, always one with a flair for the dramatic, to save his best for last.

When the 23,000 fans converged on sold-out Greensboro Coliseum the next week for the ACC Tournament, none had any way of knowing they were about to see something that had never been seen in the 41 seasons of the fabled event.

That Wake Forest won the tournament for its first ACC title in 33 years wasn't that much of a shocker, given that the Deacons were seeded No. 1. It was the way they won—no, it was the way Childress absolutely refused to let them lose—that will be forever remembered as one of the most amazing performances in conference history.

For three days, Childress owned the tournament and owned the league. In three days, Childress graduated, in the estimation of Wake Forest fans everywhere and forever, from the ranks of mere hero to that of immortal.

And at the end of those three unforgettable days, after Childress had scored more points (107) than had ever been scored in the ACC Tournament, and had done so with a dislocated pinky finger on his shooting hand, and had done so in the most dramatic fashion—by breaking the scoring record on the game-winning shot in overtime of the title game—Odom was left to concede that it was indeed Randolph Childress's world.

And the rest of us were only living in it.

Eighteen Down Against Duke

One thing about Childress: If he had something to say, he would let you hear it.

With 8:33 remaining in the first half of Wake Forest's 1995 ACC Tournament quarterfinal game against Duke, Childress was letting his teammates hear it.

In one of the most infamous timeouts in Wake Forest history, Childress let the No. 1-seeded Deacons know exactly how he felt to be trailing No. 9 seed Duke by 18 points. As embarrassed as he was irate, Childress informed everyone within the anxious circle that if they weren't going to help him win the game then just get out of his way and let him do it by himself.

"I've heard him like that before," Rusty LaRue said after the game. "He's always been kind of vocal."

Strong words can provoke strong reactions. That certainly proved to be the case on this day when the Deacons jumped on Childress's back and rode the spindly, 6-2 senior to an 87-70 victory.

Twenty seconds after play resumed from the timeout, Childress let fly a three-pointer from downtown. By the time the shot rippled the nets, the Blue Devils, whether they knew it or not, were in deep trouble.

Before the barrage was over, Childress had drained 10 straight shots on the way to a career-high 40 points. He augmented the outburst—the fifth most points scored in an ACC Tournament game—with nine assists, six rebounds and four steals. He took 18 shots from the floor and made 13. He took 12 three-pointers, and broke the ACC Tournament record by making eight.

Over one particularly torrid stretch, he scored 20 points in slightly more than eight minutes. He scored his last basket with more than four minutes remaining and left the court for good with 1:11 left.

If the game was on the line against Duke, Randolph Childress wanted to take the shot. He was a big reason why Wake Forest dominated Duke in the mid-'90s. (Courtesy of Wake Forest Media Relations)

Freshman Trajan Langdon of Duke could only shake his head in awe.

"I had seen that before, even before I got here," Langdon said. "He killed us in all three games we played him. Call him a Duke killer."

Instead of exulting in what he had accomplished, Childress was still stewing over the Deacons' start long after the game was over.

"The way we won it was not the way we played all year," Childress grumbled. "I'm still embarrassed."

A Quiet Thirty

The middle act of the three-act play in which Childress starred during the epic 1995 ACC Tournament was the least memorable. Childress scored 30 points in the Deacons' 77-68 victory over Virginia, but made only eight of 21 shots from the floor.

He did, however, hit six of the 15 three-pointers he attempted and dished out seven assists. And when the Deacons needed him most, he was there.

Wake Forest, starting slowly for the second straight day, shot 37 percent in the first half and trailed 36-28 at the break. Duncan scored the first two baskets of the second half, and Childress followed with three three-pointers in four Wake Forest possessions for a 43-40 lead.

The Cavaliers, who would get 31 points and 11 rebounds from Junior Burrough, finally faded when Harold Deane and Curtis Staples continued to misfire from the perimeter. The backcourt combo made just nine of 31 shots for the day and Wake Forest put the game away with a late 12-2 surge.

The victory guaranteed the Deacons their first appearance in the ACC finals since 1978.

"I don't know of a word to describe how bad this team wants to win," Childress said. "I'm not going to back down, and I'm not going to let my team back down."

When informed that the Deacons had not won an ACC Tournament since 1962, Childress was unfazed.

"I'm only 22," he said. "I can't speak of 30-something years."

"He Truly Is Special"

There have been so many moments since Richard Crozier introduced basketball to Wake Forest in 1906 that a follower and/or fan could count their blessings for having chosen the Deacons to be their favorite team.

But never, in the minds of many, have there been so many blessings to count as that moment with four seconds remaining in overtime of the 1995 ACC Championship game.

For it was at that moment that the 23,000-plus fans at Greensboro Coliseum witnessed first-hand one of the greatest convergences of individual accomplishment and historical significance ever in the annals of Wake Forest, the ACC and, for that matter, college basketball itself.

For it was at that moment that Randolph Childress, in his final ACC Tournament game, hit the shot that beat North Carolina 82-80, lifted Wake Forest to its first conference title in 33 years and broke a tournament scoring record that Lennie Rosenbluth of North Carolina had held since Dwight D. Eisenhower was just rolling into his second term as president in 1957.

Now there was a way to say goodbye.

"There's never been a more fitting way to end a career in the Atlantic Coast Conference Tournament," Odom observed. "Never.

"He truly is special."

In scoring 37 points, all the while playing with a dislocated pinkie on his right hand, Childress made 12 of 22 shots from the floor and nine of 17 from three-point range, and scored Wake Forest's final 14 points—five in the final two minutes of regulation and nine in overtime.

Childress won the game by flashing into the foul circle, taking a pass from Tony Rutland and sinking a 10-foot runner for a two-point lead that held up when Jerry Stackhouse of North Carolina missed a desperation three-pointer and Pierce Landry's last-gasp effort at a tip failed to fall.

"Somebody asked me if Randolph Childress had asked to take the last shot," LaRue said. "He didn't have to ask.

"We know he's going to take the last shot. That's a given."

The winning field goal gave Childress 107 points for the tournament, eclipsing the 106 points Rosenbluth had scored 38 years previously. Afterward, Childress and Odom stood on the ladder erected beneath the baskets for the net-cutting ceremony, and the coach and his star player embraced.

The victory was the Deacons' 10th straight and 24th of the season, establishing a school record for wins in a season.

One member of the losing team said it was not hard to anticipate the grand sendoff Childress gave himself from the ACC Tournament.

"It was almost like a sign of things to come when he got going against Duke," Pat Sullivan of North Carolina said, referring to Childress's 40-point barrage in the quarterfinals. "He just picked Wake Forest up on his back and carried them all the way to the ACC Championship.

"He wouldn't let Wake Forest lose. He hit the shots and showed no emotion. It was like it happened every day for somebody like that. Someday I hope to tell my kids and my grandkids that I played against someone like that."

Childress, for once, had surprisingly little to say after the game. But his performance had spoken volumes.

"I didn't want to leave and not have anything saying Wake Forest is a good basketball team," Childress said. "Having my jersey retired by the school meant a lot, but some people could look back and say, 'Well, what did Randolph Childress do for Wake Forest? He helped Wake Forest win a conference championship, which they hadn't done in quite a while.'

"That's one thing I'm very happy about."

It was a day that many people—including Coach Dean Smith of North Carolina—had cause to count their blessings.

"I congratulate him," Smith said of Childress. "I'm glad he's gone."

Timothy Ricardo LaRue?

When Odom was coaching high school baseball in his hometown of Goldsboro in 1967, his wife Lynn was expecting their first of two sons, Lane. One April day Odom was hitting infield as his team prepared for a game when the stork came winging overhead.

"My wife and my mother-in-law drove by the baseball field, and hollered out the window, 'We're going to the hospital.'" Odom recalled. "And I shouted back, 'I'll see you after the game.'"

Almost three decades later, one of Odom's players at Wake Forest was nearly faced with a similar decision. LaRue had married his high school sweetheart Tammy before his junior year at Wake Forest, and by his senior season of 1996 the couple was expecting its first child.

The due date was a subject of serious conjecture; LaRue's teammates, led by juniors Duncan and Ricardo Peral, concocted a pool to predict the impending arrival. Duncan insisted that if the new LaRue arrived on his predicted date, January 25, then the baby would have to be named for him.

"His window of opportunity is 6 a.m. to 6 p.m.," LaRue said of Duncan. "He guessed 12 o'clock, so I told him I'd give him six hours on either side. Actually it's Timothy Ricardo LaRue, after Timmy and Ricky.

"The doctor said she's not real close, so I think we're safe."

There was a question if LaRue would even be in town during the birth. The Deacons were scheduled to play at Clemson on January 21 and at North Carolina on January 27, and LaRue had already declared he didn't intend to miss a game.

His mother, Linda LaRue, was not surprised.

"I really can't imagine Rusty making it through the birth anyways," she said. "He's always almost fainted at the sight of blood. You know he's a real patsy about that."

As it turned out, LaRue was around at 4:08 a.m. on January 31, 1996 at Forsyth Baptist Hospital for the arrival of his first born. The boy, who was 21 inches long and weighed seven pounds, seven ounces, was named Riley.

"He thinks Riley will sound good over a loudspeaker one day," Tammy said of her husband.

A Scholar on Scholarship

About the time one becomes convinced that the term "student-athlete," is, if not incredible, at least inverted, along comes a remarkable person such as LaRue.

LaRue, who played quarterback for the Wake Forest football team, guard for the Deacon basketball team and even pitched three innings for the baseball team, was best known for his athletic versatility. But around Calloway Hall, where he majored in computer science, LaRue was also known as a serious and hard-working scholar.

From the summer before his freshman year of 1992-93, LaRue was involved with research financed by the National Science Foundation. One paper he co-authored at Wake Forest with Matthew Rudd—who would pursue his Ph.D. at the

University of Chicago—won a regional undergraduate award from the Sigma Xi research organization.

The title of the entry was, "An Optimization Problem in Adaptive Optics."

LaRue's mentor at Wake Forest, Dr. Robert Plemmons, knew a little about balancing the time demands of class work and athletics. During his undergraduate days at Wake Forest, from 1958 through 1961, Plemmons was a right-handed workhorse who compiled a 23-7 record for the Deacon baseball team.

After pitching for four years in the Baltimore Orioles' farm system, Plemmons earned his Ph.D. at Auburn and taught at Mississippi, Tennessee, and N.C. State before returning to his alma mater in 1991. Two years later LaRue arrived from nearby Northwest Guilford High, where, as a senior, he had passed for 1,786 yards and 18 touchdowns, averaged 25.4 points as an all-state basketball player and hit .518 while compiling an 8-2 record as a baseball player.

To the coaches at Wake Forest, LaRue's early reputation was based on his being named North Carolina's 1992 High School Athlete of the Year. Plemmons soon found out there was much more to LaRue than his ability to run, shoot and throw.

"He has been a very good student to work with—very dedicated, hard-worker, easy to get along with," Plemmons said. "I have worked with students who are brighter, but I don't think I've worked with one who is more disciplined and dedicated. Really, when you ask him to do something, he'll get it done, if it takes him all night."

LaRue graduated with honors in the spring of 1996, four years after he arrived.

Tim Shows Up

Odom knew he had strayed off the beaten path of most college coaches when he showed up one day in St. Croix, U.S. Virgin Islands to watch Duncan play.

The court at Duncan's St. Dunstan High School was outdoors, surrounded by tropical vegetation. The surface was blacktop. The backboard supports were metal and curved forward several feet to reduce the possibility of players wiping out on a fastbreak. Sea breezes from the nearby Atlantic, Caribbean air-conditioning, dried the sweat on the players faces in mid-trickle.

As he sat on a rise next to the court, Odom didn't see anything special from the players locked in competition. In fact, he didn't even see Duncan, who as a gangly 6-10, 16-year-old, was pretty much unmistakable.

"I went to a pick-up game and was just sitting there watching the players, looking for Timmy when Timmy comes up and sits down beside me," Odom recalled. "He wasn't playing. He was watching.

"I think I asked him why he wasn't out there, and Timmy told me he was waiting. He was waiting for a game or two to go by so he wouldn't get stuck on a bad team. He knew if he lost early, he'd have to sit. So he was waiting for a better team.

"He was thinking. I knew then he was smart."

Blown Off Course

Hurricane Hugo has probably been given more credit than it deserves for turning Duncan into one of the best basketball players on the planet.

The most common story of Duncan's transition from swimming to basketball has always been that after Hugo blew through in 1989, wrecking the pool in his hometown, Duncan quickly tired of training in the ocean and turned to basketball. And there is truth to the tale.

Hugo obviously did great damage to St. Croix in the Virgin Islands. The pool in which Duncan trained was destroyed. Duncan, at the time, appeared to have a brilliant future in the sport and was already ranked among the best free-style swimmers in the United States in his age group. His sister, Tricia, had represented the Virgin Islands in swimming in the 1988 Olympics in Seoul. And Duncan found the whole ordeal of trying to train in the ocean more than he wanted to deal with.

There was, however, another calamity that occurred in Duncan's life a year later that probably had at least as much effect, if not more, on diverting his career path. On April 24, 1990, the day before Duncan turned 14, his mother Delyfia died of cancer.

Delyfia had been her son's driving force, the one who encouraged him, who challenged him, who made sure he got to the meets and practices on time. His brother-in-law, Rickey Lowery, said that after she died, Duncan never swam competitively again.

"He didn't want anything to do with swimming," Lowery said. "When she left, he lost it all."

"My Heart Breaks"

The penance Dennis Felton had to pay for the sin of not being able to foresee the future was to watch a young, all-but-unknown kid from the Virgin Islands grow up to be Tim Duncan.

Felton was an assistant coach under Rick Barnes at Providence in 1993 when he came upon Duncan. Impressed by Duncan's potential, he offered him a scholarship. Duncan accepted.

As the fate of both Providence and Wake Forest basketball would have it, however, another coveted recruit also accepted an offer to play for the Friars. And Felton, to his eternal regret, had only one scholarship to give.

Felton attempted to convince Duncan to wait until spring, assuring him that another full ride would come open. But Duncan and his family were having nothing to do with the plan.

Duncan almost immediately signed with Wake Forest.

"Providence messed up," William Duncan, Tim's father, said years later. "I mean in a hurry they messed up.

"Tim was to leave tomorrow morning. They called the evening before, and they rushed the gun. They picked another guy."

The player Providence chose over Duncan was Eric Williams, not to be confused with Eric "Big E" Williams who, a decade later, would sign with Wake Forest and start at center as a freshman. This Eric Williams was an All-American at Vincennes Junior College who as a senior at Providence scored 17.7 points and grabbed 6.7 rebounds and was named first-team All-Big East.

He proved both at Providence and later in the NBA that he was a good player. But he was never NCAA Basketball's Player of the Year, nor will he, in this lifetime, be named NBA Player of the Year.

To add insult to Felton's injury, he and Barnes left Providence in 1995 to move to Clemson of the ACC, where both were reminded many, many times of what might have been.

"Now that I'm in the ACC, that's one of the hardest things I've had to deal with, seeing him on the court," Felton said in 1995, during Duncan's sophomore year. "My heart breaks every time I see him play.

"I think he'll be a Hall of Fame player."

The Third Recruit

A byproduct of the Byzantine rules of NCAA basketball is that the players at any school often know what kind of team they're going to have before the coaches do.

Players, upon returning to campus in the fall, play pickup games almost daily. Coaches, under NCAA rules, are not allowed to watch. So the upperclassmen are the first to get a read on the freshman recruits recently arrived.

There was great excitement around Wake Forest's freshman class of 1994. One recruit, Makhtar Ndiaye, was a physically developed, athletic 6-9 forward from the Senegal who was considered one of the Deacons' great gets of recent seasons. Another, Peral, was a 6-10 forward from Spain with the shooting touch of a wing guard.

And oh yeah, there was also this quiet, skinny 6-10 kid from the Virgin Islands named Duncan. Because Duncan was only 17 and had faced only nominal competition in high school, Odom and his staff were considering red-shirting him to preserve his season of eligibility.

That's until they started getting reports from the daily pickup games.

One report came from Blucas, a senior guard.

"We told the coaches, 'Don't overlook this Duncan kid,'" Blucas said. "They kept saying 'He's got a lot of growing to do. And he's only 17, he may blow out mentally.' And I'm telling them 'He's got the best timing I've ever seen.' He was blocking everybody's shots."

Another came from senior forward Trelonnie Owens.

"I told the coaches, 'Once you see this kid play, you won't be talking about redshirting,'" Owens said.

The decision, as it turned out, was made for Odom. When neither Ndiaye nor Peral were available for the opener against Alaska-Anchorage in the Great Alaska Shootout, Duncan started at center, played 10 minutes and did not score. The Deacons lost to Alaska-Anchorage, a Division II school, by the score of 70-68.

The NCAA had cautioned Wake Forest not to play Ndiaye and Peral while it investigated whether the school had violated NCAA rules in recruiting Ndiaye and whether Peral had compromised his amateur standing while playing for a professional team in Spain.

The NCAA eventually ruled against the Deacons in both cases. Wake Forest was placed on NCAA probation for its recruiting of Ndiaye—who would transfer to Michigan, and later on to North Carolina—and Peral was not allowed to play as a freshman.

When one door closes, Odom liked to say, another opens.

Odom would at times bristle at the notion that he had been one of the few not to foresee Duncan's greatness. He also disputed the common perception that Duncan, when recruited, was considered a project who after several years of development might—or might not—be able to contribute to an ACC team.

"The inference was he wasn't very good, and if he came here, he was going to have to work very hard," Odom said. "In other words it was like he was another one of Wake Forest's big guys who wasn't going to pan out.

"That was the inference. And really I think it was unfair, because no one who had written about him had ever seen him play."

But Odom also acknowledged that even a veteran coach can sometimes be surprised.

"Tim Duncan came here as a freshman recruit, the third recruit," Odom said. "He was almost the addendum. He was the dot under the exclamation point. You had Makhtar, you had Ricardo, and then you had the dot. He was the dot. He was the add-on.

"And it's turned out that he was the statement. He's ended up being the period. It didn't end, it began with him. As you look at the series of events that occurred that got him into that role, it's incredible. But it happened."

Duncan Dunks Newton

William Duncan once described his son Tim as "wise beyond his years."

Rick Lowery, Duncan's brother-in-law and mentor, said a secret to Duncan's greatness is "He controls his own atmosphere."

And, indeed, there was never a time at Wake Forest, either during a game or afterward, where he was confronted with a situation he didn't seem to know how to handle.

There was the unforgettable incident from 1996 when Greg Newton, a journeyman center for Duke, suggested that Duncan wasn't the kind of unstoppable physical force that strikes fear in the heart of opponents. Among the terms Newton used to describe Duncan were "soft," and "babyish."

In the meeting to follow, Wake Forest beat Duke 57-54 in the Blue Devils' Cameron Indoor Stadium. Duncan had 24 points and 14 rebounds and blocked four shots. Newton contributed eight points and nine rebounds to the Duke cause.

Afterward, reporters approached Duncan, informed him of Newton's comments, and asked him what he thought of the Blue Devil junior.

"He's the greatest player I've ever seen," Duncan replied.

Inadvertent Whistle

By 1994, after Duke had won its second national championship, there were ACC fans who were absolutely convinced, in their heart of hearts, that the officials favored Krzyzewski and his Blue Devils.

And it was calls like the one made on February 13, 1994 in Joel Coliseum that begged the age-old question: If a paranoid is right, is he still paranoid?

Wake Forest, at 15-7, was in dire need of a win. The second-ranked Blue Devils, at 17-2, were poised to take over the top spot since No. 1-ranked North Carolina had lost to Georgia Tech the night before.

But the Deacons weren't ready to be anybody's stepping stone. Getting stalwart performances from junior Childress (28 points), freshman Duncan (14 points, eight rebounds), senior Blucas (16 points, five rebounds) and senior Owens (12 points, nine rebounds), they led 57-54 with seven minutes remaining. Their prospects brightened considerably then when center Cherokee Parks of Duke was called for his fifth foul while reaching around Duncan in the post.

Or was he?

Official Dick Paparo, standing on the hash mark in front of the Wake Forest bench, made the call. He blew his whistle and raised his fist. But on his way to the scorers' table to report the foul, he apparently decided he hadn't seen what he had seen. He waved off the foul, leaving Parks in the game.

The reaction was both immediate and ear-splitting. As the 14,407 fans in attendance rained their boos and their food down on Paparo, one of the loudest of the loud screamed, "That was the worst call of the year."

Another official, Rick Hartzell, heard the blast.

"I didn't make it," Hartzell shrugged.

Meanwhile Paparo was trying his best to extricate himself from the furor of his own making.

"Inadvertent whistle," Paparo announced. "That's all. Inadvertent whistle."

Surprisingly little was made of Paparo's about-face. Odom was gracious after the game, as he could afford to be. Wake Forest, with Childress scoring 11 points in the final 3:49, pulled away for a 78-69 victory to secure its first regular-season sweep of Duke in 11 seasons.

Tim Just Being Tim

Besides being one of the most accomplished, fascinating and celebrated athletes to every play for Wake Forest, Tim Duncan was also one of the most enigmatic.

Even those who knew him best often had cause to wonder if they knew him at all.

During his four years at Wake Forest, no Deacon played harder or better or wanted to win more. And there was never any indication that, for his exalted status, especially during his final season or two, that Duncan was anything other than a generous and valued teammate.

Still, there was an independence about him that was at times interpreted as aloofness. Media representatives who covered Wake Forest complained how he gave his cooperation only begrudgingly. One reporter called him Mr. Eye Contact, a sarcastic reaction to Duncan's habit of looking at everything around him except the person he was addressing.

Odom realized on his recruiting visits to St. Croix that Duncan was a different kind of kid. Odom told of sitting in the Duncan living room giving his recruiting pitch while Duncan sat on the floor and played a video game on the television screen. Odom, tired of talking to the side of Duncan's head, actually sat down near the television so Duncan would at least be looking in his direction.

But Odom also realized later that Duncan, from the questions he asked, had taken in every word Odom had said.

The explanation around Wake Forest during Duncan's career was "Tim is going to do what Tim is going to do." Duncan, for his part, attributed his streak of independence to the most influential moment of his childhood, the death of his mother on April 24, 1990, the day before his 14th birthday.

"I think my Mom dying is what did that to me," Duncan said. "I love my dad, but after my Mom died, I never listened to anybody pretty much.

Tim Duncan might have been a bit enigmatic as a person, but you can't argue with his results as a player. He grabbed at least 20 rebounds in a game 10 times during his college career and set the ACC record for career blocked shots with 481. (Courtesy of Wake Forest Media Relations)

"It wasn't that I was a pain, or a problem child or anything. I just got my own views and I went with them. It's something that from that point on, it was clear to me I had to do what I wanted to do."

What made Duncan's demeanor all the more frustrating to the media covering Wake Forest was the realization that he was a terrific interview when in the mood for giving answers. He didn't waffle. He didn't hedge. He didn't say something just because it was what was supposed to be said. He told the truth. And he didn't apologize for it.

The problem was just getting him to say it.

"You Know He's There"

Of the many records Tim Duncan set at Wake Forest, the easiest to come by was probably career blocked shots.

Duncan, in retrospect, was still considered a developing big man when he blocked three shots against Winthrop in the 18th game of his sophomore season. The performance gave him a school-record 204 for his career, in just 51 college games. The previous record holder, Anthony Teachey, had blocked 203 in 121 games.

Center Todd Lassiter of Winthrop spoke for many big men of the era when he assessed Duncan's performance after the game.

"Even when he's not on you, you know he's there," Lassiter said. "He didn't block a lot of shots tonight, but when he alters a shot, it's just as good as a block."

Duncan also happened to pull down 23 rebounds in the game, won by Wake Forest 68-54. Winthrop, as a team, finished with 27 rebounds.

Mind-numbing Numbers

Lest anyone forgets just how good Tim Duncan was at Wake Forest...

No. 21 by the numbers:

128—The number of college games Duncan played.

97—The number of games Wake Forest won with Duncan on the court.

1,570—Duncan's career rebounds, third most in ACC history.

2,117—Duncan's career points, fourth most in Wake Forest history.

481—Duncan's career blocked shots, most in ACC history.

121—The number of consecutive games in which Duncan blocked at least one shot.

75—The number of times opponents shot below 40 percent from the floor.

9—The number of times opponents shot 50 percent or better from the floor.

39—The number of games in which Duncan had at least 15 rebounds.

10—The number of games in which Duncan had at least 20 rebounds.

2—The number of ACC championships Wake Forest won with Duncan at center.

1—The number of college basketball players who, when Duncan closed his Wake Forest career, had amassed at least 1,500 points, 1,000 rebounds, 400 blocked shots and 2000 assists.

Dave on the Warpath

It was late in Wake Forest's 1997 season and Odom was mad.
No, he was more than mad, he was incensed.

No, he was more than incensed, he was virtually apoplectic.

The Deacons had lost three of five games heading into the
ACC Tournament, and Odom had taken the unusual step of
closing practice to the media. But word leaked out that Odom
had kicked everybody except Tim Duncan off the starting lineup and was holding auditions during the practices leading up to
the ACC quarterfinals against Florida State.

Odom was convinced he had a mole in his office, and
threatened to fire any coach or staff member who had been the
source of the reports.

One reporter who had written the account was Al
Featherston of the *Durham Herald-Sun*. On seeing Featherston
in Greensboro on Thursday, the day before the Tournament
would begin, Odom interrogated Featherstone about where he
had gotten the information.

"I got it from you," Featherston said. "You talked about it
on your radio show Monday night."

"No I didn't," Odom responded.

"Yes you did," Featherston said. "Others heard it too."

Odom then turned to John Justus, the Wake Forest Sports
Information Director standing nearby.

"Is that true?" Odom asked Justus.

Justus confirmed it was.

"Well," said Odom. "I guess I just scooped myself."

A Sad Coincidence

Three of the best big men to ever play in the Atlantic Coast
Conference played for Wake Forest. But all those years
when they haven't had Dickie Hemric, Len Chappell or Duncan

dominating the lane, the Deacons have generally remained in the thick of things in the conference because of tough, competitive guards who could control the ebb and flow of a game and hit a timely jumper in the clutch.

Jackie Murdock, Billy Packer, Dave Wiedeman, Charlie Davis, Skip Brown, Frank Johnson, Danny Young, Delaney Rudd, Muggsy Bogues, Childress, Justin Gray and Chris Paul— you can click them off like freight cars at a railway crossing.

Thus, one of the saddest coincidences ever in Wake Forest history is that when the Deacons ended up with the hands-down best player in college basketball, Odom got caught without a backcourt capable of capitalizing on Duncan's legendary abilities. It's not that Odom didn't have a topflight guard to play with Duncan, he just didn't have one after the final game of Rutland's sophomore season.

For by the middle of that season, Rutland, a 6-2 sharpshooter from Hampton, Virginia, was coming on strong. And by the championship of the ACC Tournament, when the Deacons were playing Georgia Tech for their second straight league crown, he was playing at least stride for stride with freshman Stephon Marbury of the Yellow Jackets.

"I can still see the first half and the first two or three minutes of the second half of the ACC final of his sophomore year, in a game he was faced with Stephon Marbury being his opposing guard," Odom said two years later. "I looked out there and really had questions about which was the better one. They were both very, very good."

There was a wistful tone to Odom's voice, because of what happened in those first minutes of the second half. Driving to the basket on a fast break, Rutland slipped and tore a ligament in his knee.

Wake Forest led 49-31 at the time, and Rutland had scored 15 points by hitting five of seven three-pointers. After the Deacons managed to hold on desperately for a 75-74 victory, Coach Bobby Cremins of Georgia Tech revealed one of the most advanced cases of myopia in ACC history.

What, Cremins was asked, was the impact of Rutland's injury on the game?

"Was Rutland hurt?" Cremins wondered. "When was he hurt?"

It would be overstating the case to say Rutland was never again any good. He averaged 11.8 points as a junior and 12.7 as a senior, and finished his career ranked 19th on Wake Forest's all-time scoring list with 1,274 points.

But he wasn't ever again as good as he appeared he was going to be. And when it mattered most, he wasn't as good as he needed to be to help lead the Deacons to the Final Four.

He missed the last two games of Wake Forest's NCAA Tournament run in 1996, including the 83-63 loss to Kentucky in the final of the Midwest Regional. And he was outplayed badly by Brevin Knight of Stanford in the second round of the 1997 NCAA Tournament, when he made only five of 14 shots in a 72-66 loss that ended Duncan's career.

"I always wish for what would have happened if I hadn't gotten injured," Rutland said during his senior season. "Because I was starting to play some great ball, and who knows what would have happened my junior year, or if I would have been here my senior year."

Odom was criticized for playing Rutland the first two games of the 1996 NCAA Tournament, against Northeast Louisiana and Texas, though he maintained he had been assured Rutland could not further aggravate the injury. But even he wondered aloud later if Rutland came back too soon. "Perhaps we would have been better served giving him a year off, I don't know," Odom said in 1998. " I'm not questioning that. That was his decision, and it was my decision. The doctors said he was OK. And he actually played pretty well as a junior, considering that."

A Father Looks Up at His Son

Leaving home for school is rarely easy.
For Darius Songaila, it was one of the hardest things he'll ever do.

A native of Marijampole, Lithuania, Songaila didn't have to leave just his hometown, but his homeland as well when he decided to attend New Hampton Institute in New Hampshire. For all the opportunity he knew he was being afforded, he rued the day he had to tell his father, Ignas, that he was leaving.

Like most sons, Songaila looked up to his father. But his father also looked up to him, and had to from the day he was paralyzed from a fall at a construction site and confined to a wheelchair.

"It made it tougher," Songaila said. "He wasn't an old guy. It wasn't like he'd been through life and had nothing else to see. He was 50. Then you don't have your legs."

Making the parting all the more difficult was their mutual love for fishing. Only with Darius around could Ignas go fishing, because Darius was the only person around big and strong enough to lift his father from the wheelchair and carry him down to the water.

Darius said his father understood his reasons for leaving home for the United States. But that didn't stop the tears from falling.

Songaila, who scored 1,859 points and pulled down 813 rebounds for Wake Forest from 1999 through 2002, proved he made the right decision. After playing with Moscow in the European Professional League in 2003, he played for the Sacramento Kings of the NBA in 2004.

But just because a decision's right doesn't necessarily make it easy.

"We Can't Hold Him"

For a prospector, as all college basketball recruiters have to be, finding gold doesn't guarantee riches. Sometimes the problem is getting the gold from the ground to the bank.

That's what Lane Odom came to realize when he was a young assistant coach at East Carolina. While scouting New Hampton Institute in New Hampshire, he realized he had come across a real prospect when he first saw the new kid from Lithuania named Darius Songaila.

At first he allowed himself to envision what a 6-9, 250-pound recruit like Songaila could do for the East Carolina program. But his euphoria began to fade when he saw more and more coaches from more established programs beginning to take note of Songaila as well.

That's when he placed a call to his father, Dave, who was head coach at the time at Wake Forest.

Odom said: "He called me and said, 'Dad I just saw Darius play and you'd better get over to take a look at him. We're still going to recruit him, but if big schools start messing with him, and we can't hold him, you ought to be in position to do something.'"

Odom and the Deacons' recruiting coordinator, Frank Haith, quickly moved into position and harvested the gold that Lane Odom had first laid eyes upon. A year later, as a freshman, Songaila averaged 12.1 points and 5.3 rebounds for Wake Forest.

Chapter 7
A New Century

From a Lark to a Career

It would be accurate, if a bit misleading, to say that coaching basketball was Skip Prosser's chosen profession. But Wake Forest's basketball coach didn't choose it. It was chosen for him.

A graduate of the U.S. Merchant Marine Academy, Prosser majored in, as he called it, driving ships. The actual degree was Nautical Science.

Though for the most part, he enjoyed his time in the academy, he didn't like the two six-month stints on the high seas enough to spend his life onboard ships. His aunt, who lived in Wheeling, West Virginia, mentioned him to a headmaster at a school there called Linsly Institute.

"I went down to interview sort of on a lark," Prosser said. "I figured there was no way I was going to get this job.

"But they said, 'As long as you're working toward your education degree, and your certification, we'll hire you as a teacher. But you have to coach ninth-grade basketball, and you have to help out with ninth-grade football.' So I did.

"That's how I got into coaching. I had no choice. If I wanted a teaching job, I had to take the coaching job."

It didn't take Prosser long to realize what a tough gig coaching can be. In his first game, his ninth-grade team trailed 16-0 at the end of the first quarter.

"It was 22-zip before my team ever scored."

Prosser's first team rallied to finish 7-8, and he soon found how much he liked the job. That said, he hardly followed a fast track to college basketball, instead spending four years as a ninth-grade coach, one coaching junior varsity and eight as a high school coach—two seasons at Linsly and six at Central Catholic High School in Wheeling.

He was successful enough at Central Catholic to post a 104-48 record, and win the 1982 state 2A championship with a 25-2 record. But it was his friendship with Pete Gillen, who by 1998 was coaching in the ACC at Virginia, that paved his way into the college game.

Prosser got to know Gillen when Gillen was an assistant coach at VMI scouting players in Wheeling. He got to know him better while observing at the prestigious Five-Star All-Star camp, first in Wheeling and later when the camp moved to Pittsburgh.

After Gillen had become head coach at Xavier by 1984, Prosser was told he needed an assistant.

"He got real desperate," Prosser said. "He offered the job to three guys, Bob Hurley, Sr., a guy named Pat Knapp and a guy named Happy Dobbs. They all said 'No.'

"He said 'Call me at 6 o'clock Friday.' I was scouting a football game for the (Central Catholic) varsity coach and I called Coach Gillen from a phone booth on Ohio Route 7, in Powhatan Point, Ohio. My phone booth was shaking. The semis were going by. It was a two-lane.

"He said, 'Can you recruit?' I said, 'Sure.' I had no idea. And he hired me."

The Mangler Gets Married

By late in Darius Songaila's junior season, rumors were rampant that he would leave Wake Forest and return to his native Lithuania to play in the European professional leagues. Though a powerful force inside, Songaila was considered by many around Wake Forest and the Atlantic Coast Conference to be a marked man in the eyes of the officials.

There were those who traced Songaila's treatment from the officials to a postgame comment by Gillen of Virginia.

"He's a mangler," Gillen said. "He kills innocent bystanders sometimes in the post."

Over 130 career games, Songaila was whistled for 436 fouls, for an average of 3.4 per game. He fouled out 24 times.

In an 82-80 home loss to Duke in 2001, a game that television commentator Billy Packer described as "The roughest game I've seen in a long time," center Rafael Vidaurreta of Wake Forest was called for three fouls in 34 minutes, center Carlos Boozer of Duke was called for three fouls in 30 minutes and forward Shane Battier of Duke was called for one foul in 39 minutes. Songaila, in the meantime, was tagged with four fouls in 13 minutes of action.

After another game, an 81-71 loss at Maryland the same season, Coach Dave Odom perhaps unwittingly fueled the rumors of Songaila's imminent departure after watching his star center sit most of the game in foul trouble.

"Darius Songaila, my friends, if I were him I would pack up and go home," Odom lamented. "That's what I would do. I'd pack up and go home."

As Wake Forest beat reporter for the *Winston-Salem Journal*, I asked Songaila on a number of occasions if he would indeed be back for his senior season. Though very approachable and patient by nature, Songaila finally tired of being asked the same question over and over.

In an effort to debunk the rumors for once and for all, Songaila explained why he would indeed be back for his senior season. He was engaged by then to Jackie Houston, a one-time tennis player at Wake Forest, and he wanted his parents to be on hand from Lithuania for two grand occasions.

"I want to bring my parents here for graduation," Songaila said. "It's going to be May, and I'm going to be out of school, so (the wedding) is going to be around that time.

"It's expensive to bring my family back and forth a few times. So I'm just planning to do it at that time."

Songaila appeared a bit sheepish the next time I saw him. His finance, he explained, wasn't very happy with him. Although there was no secret the two were engaged, they had yet to formally announce the date of the marriage when it was printed on the sports pages of the *Winston-Salem Journal*.

Thankfully, Songaila forgave me, just as Jackie forgave him. The two were married after his graduation in the spring of 2002.

Josh the Truth-sayer

Ralph Waldo Emerson, an essayist, poet and philosopher often quoted by Prosser, once observed that "The greatest homage to the truth is to tell it."

If so, then probably no Deacon alive or dead ever paid more homage to the truth than Josh Howard.

Howard could be truthful to a fault. The word around Wake Forest during the four years Howard played for the Deacons was, if you don't want the truth, don't ask Josh a question.

In the final moments of my first really extensive interview with Howard, during his sophomore season of 2001, I just happened to ask, by way of conversation more than anything else, about the morale on the team. He surprised me with the truth, saying that some of his teammates were sniping at each other.

Immediately I found Coach Dave Odom and told him how Howard had called his teammates out. Odom, given time to collect his thoughts, replied that Howard should be commended for telling it like he saw it. The Deacons, shortly thereafter, started winning again, and Howard's words were seen by some as a turning point in the season.

Ernie Nestor, an assistant coach at Wake Forest for 14 seasons under Carl Tacy and Dave Odom, told of the award a local civic organization gave Howard early in his career at Wake Forest. There were two functions planned, a luncheon and an awards banquet.

When Nestor accompanied Howard to the banquet, an organizer greeted them warmly and told Howard how honored the group was to have him.

"I'm sure you just got so busy you weren't able to attend the luncheon," the person said.

The world is filled with people would have gratefully seized the excuse. But there are only so many Josh Howards.

"No," Howard replied. "I just forgot."

A Professor in His Face

B ecause Wake Forest has an undergraduate enrollment of less than 4,000, the intimacy of the university affords a more personal relationship between students and professors. As a freshman, Howard found one relationship with one professor to be a little more personal than he expected.

Howard has always been a proud and emotional individual, and early in his career he allowed his emotions to result in regrettable confrontations with opposing players and officials. After one such incident, he found an angry professor in his face.

Dr. Herman Eure, the chairman of Wake Forest's biology department, and a black man himself, had taken offense at Howard's on-court comportment.

"It incensed the hell out of me," Eure said. "I went the next week to find him. I ran into him, and told him who I was.

I said, 'Now you don't know me from Adam, and you can tell me to go to hell once I leave and everything is fine. But the behavior you exhibited the other night was embarrassing to me as a black man. You do not have to respond that way.' He stood there, and he listened, and he acknowledged it.

"After that point, he and I talked a great deal, and I invited him to my house. He's a good young man. I could tell that."

A War of Wills

The name Erika Harrison cannot be found in any record books of Wake Forest basketball, but in the spring of 2000 she was responsible for one of the biggest assists in Howard's career.

Howard, as a freshman, struggled academically, so much so that Jane Caldwell, the Deacons' director of academic counseling, wondered if Howard would survive the classroom rigors to remain eligible in basketball.

"He fought me every inch of the way academically, his first year here," Caldwell said. "Honestly, it was a huge struggle."

The war of wills reached the point that one day Howard walked out of a study hall and headed away from campus, planning never to return. And Caldwell was not inclined to try to change his mind.

"I had just made him so mad," Caldwell said. "I laid it on the line.

"I had kind of gotten to the point where I said, 'I've given too much effort for someone not to care. Now you need to make a decision.' He walked out on study hall and he walked out on me."

That's when Harrison came through for her school and Howard, the person, as well as the player. Harrison, then a student serving as an academic tutor, chased Howard down, convinced him to reassess his circumstances, and talked him into remaining at Wake Forest.

"The one thing I told him was to definitely take advantage of the opportunity," Harrison said. "No one really knows the magnitude of his genuineness and the magnitude of the level of intelligence he has. He has one of the most practical senses of intelligence that anyone at Wake Forest could ever want to have."

The story ended happily, with Howard walking across the stage on May 19, 2003 to receive a diploma denoting a degree in Religion from Wake Forest University.

A Great Group Hug

In the summer of 2003, I was assigned by the *Winston-Salem Journal* to write a story on where Howard was drafted by the NBA and the reaction from Howard and others in the Wake Forest program.

After arranging to spend the evening watching the draft on television with Howard at the home of his mother, Nancy Henderson, I was told by Wake Forest personnel that the plans had been changed. The agents representing Howard overruled the original arrangement, perhaps protecting Howard from the possibility of his not being picked in the first round.

My only recourse was to watch the show at my home, and drive to Mrs. Henderson's home, some 15 minutes away, as soon as Howard was picked.

Those representing Howard had expressed confidence that Howard would be drafted somewhere between New Orleans' pick at No. 18, and the Los Angeles Lakers' pick at No. 24. The evening looked bleak for Howard when the 25th pick arrived, and he had still not been drafted.

One team that had expressed no interest in Howard, I had been told by one of Howard's agents, was the Dallas Mavericks, the team that owned the 29th and final pick of the first round. So after the San Antonio Spurs used the No. 28 pick to select Leandrinho Barbosa of Brazil, I headed out the door.

I was en route when I caught the tail-end of a bulletin from ESPN radio that "The Dallas Mavericks, with the final pick of the first round of the NBA draft, have selected Josh Howard of Wake Forest."

I arrived at Mrs. Henderson's home about five minutes later to find a sizeable media contingency vastly outnumbered by Howard's friends, family and well-wishers. The relief was palpable, greater, perhaps, than even the realization that Howard's lifelong dream had been fullfilled. As a first-round pick, he was guaranteed a three-year contract.

Howard stood in the cul-de-sac in front of his mother's home and answered questions. He had clearly been crying, as had many of the family who now poured out of the house to celebrate the moment.

When Howard's name was announced, I was told, 40 people swarmed to hug Howard at once. But the hug he said he would never forget was that of his grandmother, Helen Howard, who raised him.

"It was overwhelming—I couldn't believe it at first," Howard said.

"It struck me when I hugged my grandmother I grew up with.

"Yeah that was a big feeling.

"It's Like I was in Survivor"

There are clearly worse places to be stranded than the verdant, shady campus of Wake Forest University.

But as a young stranger in a strange land thousands of miles from home, Vytas Danelius of Kaunas, Lithuania was sending out distress signals.

In stark contrast to his reputation with the refs, Darius Songaila earned a much different reputation with teammate Vytas Danelius— that of a caring big brother. (AP/WWP)

Two such signals showed up on the cell phone of Songaila upon his arrival back on campus for his senior season. The messages were straight and to the point.

From one Lithuanian to another, help.

"I said, 'Darius, I have no blankets, no nothing.'" Danelius recalled. "I was sleeping on that mattress. My room was empty. I had nothing. I said, 'Help me.'

"The first day we went to the mall, and we bought everything I needed, food and all. It was really a relief. It's like I was in *Survivor*."

Despite the difference in class and age, the senior Songaila and freshman Danelius struck up a friendship that helped Danelius through the trying transition into big-time college basketball. Songaila had his circle of friends at Wake, as Danelius was soon to develop, but around the Miller Center where the Deacons practice, it was rare to see one without the other.

"I can't imagine being here as a freshman without Darius," Danelius said. "I would say he's kind of my older brother."

But there was only so much the older brother was willing to do. When it came to affairs of the heart, Songaila quickly let Danelius know he was on his own.

"He can't count on me for everything," Songaila said. "I can give him some pillows, but I can't bring him girls and say, 'Here you go.' That's something he has to do.

"I think part of it is that he's a little bit shy, maybe— around girls especially."

Defending the Home Turf

Danelius has been fortunate enough to win most of his home games during his career at Wake Forest. As a freshman, the Deacons were 13-3 in Joel Coliseum. As a sophomore, they ran the table at 16-0. And as a junior, the Deacons won 12 and lost three.

Of course, there's probably no one who has ever played at Wake Forest who knows more about the importance of defending the home turf than Vytas Danelius.

He was eight years old when his hometown of Kaunas, Lithuania was occupied by troops from the collapsing Soviet Union. Tanks rumbled down the street outside his home, and he and his brother didn't know where their parents were.

He would come to learn that his father Algirdas, a pediatric neurosurgeon, and his mother Violetta, a general practitioner, were demonstrating against the invasion.

"It was scary," Danelius recalled. "I didn't know what was happening. I looked through the window, and I saw the tanks and the other military forces. They were on the street. Nobody told me what was happening, and then I understood.

"Me and my brother, we said, 'Where are my dad and mom?' Everybody went to the capitol and gathered in the parliament.

"In the middle of the night, I woke up. There were sirens, because the Russians were occupying. The military forces were overtaking the TV towers, the parliament, the radio station. They were shooting at people. They were driving tanks on live bodies. I saw this on TV, and I was scared."

Vytas's parents survived the upheaval, as did his three brothers. For that matter, so did his home country. Lithuania, which had been dominated politically and militarily for five centuries by Russia, Poland, Germany and the Soviet Union, was in September 1992 recognized as a free state, becoming the first of the satellite nations to break away from the U.S.S.R.

"The occupation showed that nothing comes easy," Danelius said. "You have to fight for yourselves. It was challenging, but Lithuania was the first country to get out from under the Soviets."

"Funnest Game I've Ever Played"

It was the eve of St. Valentine's Day, 2003, and Wake Forest fans were madly in love with their team.

They showed their affections storming out of their seats and transforming the playing surface of Joel Coliseum into one giant mosh pit. Freshman Trent Strickland pitched across the human wave like a piece of driftwood, his limbs spread and his face wearing an expression of ecstasy. Few celebrations in school history have been wilder.

Anyone wondering just how much frustration can build with 14 straight losses to an opponent got their answer when the Deacons, led by freshmen Strickland and Justin Gray and sophomores Danelius and Jamaal Levy, beat Duke 94-80 in double overtime. In a battle-royal that featured 64 fouls, 76 free throws and eight disqualifications, Wake Forest beat the Blue Devils for the first time since Tim Duncan's senior season of 1997.

"This game will go down in history," freshman Eric Williams gushed. "It was intense. That had to be the funnest game I've ever played in my life."

The Deacons, who had suffered a heartbreaking home loss to the Blue Devils two seasons before, had reason to wonder when they would ever climb out from under Duke's thumb. They had a chance to win at the end of regulation, but Gray missed a jumper. They had an even better chance to win at the end of the first overtime, but Levy left a point-blank follow shot on the front of the rim.

"When we had a couple of opportunities to win at the end of the first overtime, it looked like bad karma there," Prosser said. "But somehow, some way, we managed to get the win."

Gray, one month and one day before, had suffered a broken jaw after coming out on the short end of a pick by the Blue Devils' Dahntay Jones. In his first game back, Gray retaliated with 18 points. He delivered two of the game's biggest baskets, a three-pointer with 13 minutes remaining in regulation that cut the Duke lead to 53-48 and another three-point basket that pulled Wake Forest to 63-61 with 8 1/2 minutes left.

"If you want to point out one guy, point out Justin Gray," Coach Mike Krzyzewski of Duke said. "He hadn't played in a month and he got 18 points.

"Gray looked like a very mature player, very poised out there. And that helped them immensely, his play."

In the second overtime, however, the Deacons rode the fresh legs of Strickland to victory. After a free throw by Jones gave Duke its last lead at 75-74, Strickland scored in the lane to ignite a game-breaking 12-0 run.

Strickland scored 10 of his 12 points in the second overtime. His outburst helped overcome a rare sub-par performance by Howard, who fouled with 4:54 left in regulation having scored just 10 points.

"I was just thinking about Josh after he fouled out," Strickland said. "He was telling me he had never won against Duke since he's been here. I just wanted to step up and play the role he played when he was out there and do the best I could.

"I was kind of hoping this would happen for me, but also I was kind of afraid because it would be my first time in this situation. But everything went well."

A Typical Pittsburgh Guy

Coaching college basketball is a tough business. Some college coaches command a king's salary, but they earn every penny. They work seven days a week, and would work eight if the calendar allowed it. They're judged two or three times a week by a giant scoreboard in front of thousands, if not millions, of people.

So, though he rarely shows it to the public at large, Prosser of Wake Forest can be a tough guy.

And he came by his toughness honestly.

Coach Prosser adopted his competitiveness at an early age from his father, who told him that it's not stated in the rule book that a team can't win them all. (AP/WWP)

Prosser's father George worked for many years on the Pennsylvania Railroad. But he also found time to coach Little League baseball, and one of his players was his son Skip.

Skip ran to first base one game and tripped over the bag. His arm was throbbing when he returned to the bench.

"I was a kid, 12 years old," Prosser recalled. "I went up to him and said, 'My arm hurts.' I was almost crying.

"He goes, 'Well you've got one on the other side, don't you?' I said, 'yeah.' So I went out and played two or three innings. I remember hitting the ball and I remember catching a grounder."

When the game was over, father took son by the hospital for X-rays that confirmed that the son's arm was broken.

"I was done for the year," Prosser said. "Nowadays you would sue him for child endangerment.

"That's the way he was."

Another time Skip came home from a bitter one-run loss, and was so mad he threw his glove into a chair. His mom attempted to console him by telling him that nobody wins them all.

"My old man said, 'It don't say that in the rule book,'" Skip said. "And he's right. It doesn't say that in the rule book. You can win them all.

"That was just his attitude."

Years later, when Prosser first left home to attend the Merchant Marine Academy in Kings Point, N.Y., he was having a difficult transition from one phase of his life to the next. He became so miserable, in fact, that he called home and told his father that he was leaving the academy to return to Pittsburgh.

Prosser recalled: "He said, 'Well, if you come home I don't know where you're going to sleep. Because as soon as we get off the phone I'm going to go upstairs and knock your bed apart.'

"So I decided to stay."

When Childress Became a Verb

B us trips, even those as short as the two hours it takes to commute from Winston-Salem to Raleigh, can be dull, boring events for restless, highly active college basketball players.

The prevailing mood of the Deacons as they departed Winston-Salem on March 7, 2003, however, could best be described as tense. Wake Forest was scheduled to play at N.C. State the next day, and all that was riding on the Deacons as they rode to Raleigh was a chance to clinch an outright first-place finish in the ACC regular season for the first time since 1962.

Realizing, perhaps, that his team needed some entertainment to cut through the strain, Prosser had a video shown of the Deacons' 82-80 overtime victory over North Carolina in the championship of the 1995 ACC Tournament.

Prosser, when he first came to Wake Forest, said he didn't know all that much about Randolph Childress, who graduated six seasons before Prosser arrived. But Prosser got a good look that day at Childress and what he meant to the Deacons program. And it wasn't just the 37 points Childress scored, or the winning basket he sank, that convinced Prosser that Childress was a player he would have loved to have coached.

The Deacons were losing to the Tar Heels when a teammate made a turnover. The courtside microphone picked up Childress telling the teammate, in graphic, but certainly no-uncertain, terms, to give him the ball, on every play. Coaches like take-charge guys who take charge when it matters most.

The favorite moment for the players—and the one they demanded be replayed over and over—was Childress's cross-over dribble performed so adroitly that the player guarding him, Jeff McInnis, stumbled and fell to the hardwood. Childress first motioned McInnis to get up, then drained another jumper.

Gray grew up in Charlotte just down the street from McInnis, and remembers the play vividly.

"When I was growing up, Jeff was my idol," Gray said. "I was going 'Get him, Jeff, get him, Jeff—oooh, get up, Jeff.'"

Gray said that, to this day, Randolph Childress is a sore subject for McInnis.

"If you mention Randolph or Childress in his presence, it is an argument waiting to happen," Gray said. "I went home in the summer and I told him, 'I can't wait to play Carolina. I'm going to Childress somebody.'"

Prosser's tactics worked. Wake Forest beat N.C. State the next day, with Gray hitting three momentum-turning three-pointers to help rally the Deacons to a 78-72 victory.

Hanging Out with the Deacons

Sportswriters visiting Wake Forest to research articles on the Deacons are invariably stunned by how available they find Prosser and the players to be. Prosser is a rarity as a head coach in Division I basketball, in that he still opens his practices to the media.

One reporter once quizzed Prosser on his open-door policy.

Prosser replied that as a high school coach, he appreciated those coaches who allowed him to drop in and observe. He also said he trusted the media to not write anything he felt shouldn't be in the newspaper.

"And if we get burned," Prosser said. "We'll close practice."

It's obvious to anyone on hand how much Prosser and his assistants enjoy being on the court working with the players. Prosser showed up at one early-morning practice over the Christmas holidays bursting with such energy that I couldn't help but laugh.

"You love this, don't you?" I said.

"What? Being in the gym?" he replied. "It beats being at the mall."

Observers also might be surprised to see how much Prosser delegates to his assistant coaches, Dino Gaudio, Jeff Battle and Chris Mack. He has been known to drift over and chat with visitors while one of the other coaches conducts a drill.

One day, stung by criticism of an article I had written, I happened to say to Prosser, "Boy the fans, they really get all over us sometimes."

Prosser gave me a wry look.

"Like they don't jump all over me?" he replied.

"Yeah, but there's one big difference," I came back. "You make 10 times more money than I do."

Prosser thought about that for maybe a second.

"You're right," he said.

Then he went back to coaching his team.

Aunt Rhonda Has a Better Idea

Wake Forest fans didn't need to see Chris Paul play as a freshman in the 2004 season to know he was special. There was a tragedy that occurred Paul's senior year at crosstown West Forsyth High School that told them all they would need to know about Paul the player, and Paul the person.

The Pauls of Lewisville, North Carolina are an extremely close family. They've been known to fill pretty much a whole row of a theatre as Chris, brother C.J. and friends would sit next to their parents, Charles and Robin, watching a movie.

That's why the phone call Chris received on November 15, 2002, while attending a high school football game, was the one he will never forget. His beloved grandfather Nathaniel Jones, Robin's father, had been ambushed by five teenage boys while walking into his home. They taped his mouth shut, tied his hands behind his back, and beat him to death.

Chris worshipped his grandfather, the man everyone called "Chili." Nathaniel Jones owned and operated a Chevron station close to the Wake Forest campus, and every day when he reported to work at 6 a.m., he phoned Chris and C.J. to get them up and about and ready for school.

"My grandfather was my best friend," Paul said.

The brutality and finality of the murder rocked Paul so badly he contemplated giving up the game he loved almost as much as his grandfather. An aunt, Rhonda Richardson, had a better idea.

Why not score 61 points in your next game, Aunt Rhonda suggested, one for each year of Nathaniel Jones's life?

"I thought it was impossible," Paul recalled. "The most points I had ever scored in a game was 39."

Paul described the game, the opener of his senior season, as one might describe an out-of-body experience. He could do no wrong. He would take an off-balance shot and the ball would fly straight through the net. The points piled up until late in the fourth quarter he looked up to find his family in the stands.

They held two fingers aloft. He needed two points to score 61.

Paul drove the lane and made the layup as he was drawing a foul. He went to the free-throw line, intentionally missed the free throw by simply throwing the ball out of bounds, and removed himself from the game.

The West Forsyth Titans won the game 117-71.

"I walked out, looked at my dad, and started crying," Paul said.

"That's the Kind of Kid He Is"

An appendectomy is generally not an elective surgery. There was reason to wonder if that might change after Taron Downey's performance against Memphis in the opener of the 2003-04 season.

"Coach Prosser has been talking about it," Williams said. "He said that since Taron played this well, we all might have to get something done to ourselves that makes us play like he did."

Downey, the Deacons' junior guard, fell ill on the evening of November 4. Soldiering on, he and Paul met with school children the next day as part of Wake Forest's community service program. But Downey continued to feel bad, and finally, after consulting with trainer Greg Collins, was admitted to Wake Forest University Baptist Medical Center where, that evening his appendix was removed.

He said he would be recovered by the Deacons' opener on November 13, a prediction that seemed a bit optimistic at the time.

He was released from the hospital November 6.

He dressed for practice on November 10, but did little other than shoot a few baskets.

He practiced some on November 11, but was held out of any drills involving contact.

He flew with the team on November 12 and survived a turbulent flight that required the plane to be re-routed to a small airport a couple of hours north of New York City.

He dressed for the game against Memphis, and, to the surprise of many, entered the fray after the first media timeout with 15:06 left in the first half. With sophomore guard Gray in foul trouble, Downey played 11 minutes in the first half.

He re-entered the game with 18:20 remaining, and played the rest of the way. Showing no ill effects, Downey scored a career-high 20 points by making seven of 11 shots from the floor—including four three-pointers in the second half that carried the Deacons' to an 85-76 victory.

"Taron Downey, I thought, played with tremendous courage tonight," Prosser said afterward. "Early in the game I kept asking him if he wanted to come out. At the end of the game I decided not to ask him anymore.

"And if he wanted to come out, I probably would have ignored him anyway."

Downey confessed he surprised even himself by playing 29 minutes.

"To tell you the truth I didn't think I was going to play that many minutes at all, because I was out of shape," Downey said. "Coach has been working with me after practice and I was dogging it. But I just came and I played.

"The adrenaline kept me going."

Downey taught all his teammates a thing or two about toughness that night, a lesson that was not lost on a teammate playing his first college game.

"He meant everything to this win," Paul said. "We weren't sure Taron was going to even play a second. If Taron Downey doesn't play this game tonight, our win is questionable.

"He stepped it up big time."

One for the Ages

By the time Paul, Kyle Visser and Todd Hendley returned from Wake Forest's road trip to North Carolina on December 20, 2003, the three Deacon freshmen had played but one ACC game in their lives.

The first experience of anything is often an experience easy to remember. In remembering this experience, the trio will have plenty of company.

For no one who saw this game, either live at the Smith Center or on television, is likely to soon forget the Deacons' 119-114 triple overtime victory in what many who had been around for decades were calling one of the greatest games in the history of the ACC.

"I told the kids before the game, 'This is one of those games you're going to remember for the rest of your life.'" Prosser said. "I wish I was that accurate about everything.

"Because this is certainly one for the ages."

North Carolina, having lost its previous four games against Wake Forest, was spoiling for revenge. Coach Roy Williams had at long last been wooed away from Kansas to lead the North Carolina program out of its own version of the basketball wilderness and the Tar Heels were ranked No. 4 with a 6-0 record.

The Deacons, also 6-0, were ranked No. 14.

The Tar Heels made three concentrated thrusts to break Wake Forest's resolve. The first came in the opening five minutes when North Carolina surged to a 19-8 lead. The second took place midway through the second half when the Tar Heels barged ahead 69-62. And the third was made in the third overtime, when North Carolina grabbed a 111-107 lead on a dunk by Jawad Williams.

Even after losing Paul, their celebrated freshman, to five fouls in the second overtime, the Deacons declined to go quietly into the chilly pre-Christmas night. Downey stabbed the Tar Heels with a dagger-like three-pointer from the right wing and

Visser, playing like a fourth-year senior, tapped in a teammate's miss to vault the Deacons into a 112-111 lead.

Then Williams, known to his teammates as Big E, put the big exclamation point on the proceedings by scoring six of the game's final nine points to finish with a career-high 24 points. After Strickland slapped the ball away from North Carolina's Raymond Felton with the Deacons leading 117-114, Williams, a 63-percent free-throw shooter, made two fouls shots with two seconds remaining for the final margin.

"It was a very disappointing game for us, to say the least," said a somber Roy Williams. "And it's got to be very exhilarating for Wake Forest.

"They have to have a phenomenal feeling right now to go through that."

As the Deacons raised their fists in triumph, records fell.

Never before had North Carolina scored 100 points in a game and lost.

Never before had Wake Forest scored that many points on the road.

Never before had North Carolina played, much less lost, a multiple-overtime game in the Smith Center.

Never before had Wake Forest scored more than 103 points against a ranked opponent.

Not since 1989, when the Deacons lost to N.C. State 110-103 in four overtimes, had Wake Forest played as long a game.

And only once before, when Maryland beat N.C. State 124-110 in 1978, had an ACC game produced more points. The date of that barn-burner, coincidentally, was also December 20.

Seven players scored at least 10 points for the Deacons, who shot 51 percent and made just 16 turnovers in 55 minutes. Six players scored at least 10 points for the Tar Heels, who shot 49 percent and made just 15 turnovers in 55 minutes.

"There were just so many big plays," Prosser said. "It was unbelievable.

"Somebody would make a big play, and when somebody answered, you weren't even surprised. You just said, 'Well, there was another great play.'"

Visser, who rose to the occasion to score 13 points and pull down eight rebounds, appeared far more dazed after the game than he had during.

"It was a great game to be in, whether you win or lose," he said. "The atmosphere was unbelievable.

"I don't know if I can handle that 15 more times this season."

Justin Comes Through

Part of the educational process of most college basketball players is dealing with the media. Some players see it as something to tolerate. With a roll of the eyes, or a sigh, they let you know.

Perhaps it's because they're not inundated with as many requests as players at other, larger schools, but the basketball players at Wake Forest are generally recognized as among the friendliest and most cooperative in the ACC. As the beat reporter of the *Winston-Salem Journal*, I'm lucky in that regard. And I know it.

Some of the Deacons actually seem to relish their relationships with members of the media. Few have been more natural at being interviewed than Gray, another of the many ways he reminds long-time Wake Forest observers of Randolph Childress—a media darling of the mid-90s.

Before Wake Forest traveled to play SMU on December 15, 2003, Gray was in a bit of a slump, having made only three of 13 three-pointers in the previous two games. But I wrote my advance to the game on how Gray was absolutely certain he was posed to break out.

The first four paragraphs read as follows:

Wake Forest fans hope to see plenty more of this in 2004-05—Justin Gray embracing Chris Paul after a big win. (AP/WWP)

"His shot's not quite there, but guard Justin Gray of Wake Forest says it's close.

"Really close.

"So close he can feel it.

"'It's right there,' Gray said. 'I've had a lot rim in and rim out.'"

True to his word, Gray hit six three-pointers in the first half and had 20 points by halftime. The Deacons beat the Mustangs 78-66.

Before Wake Forest's next practice, I congratulated Gray on both his rediscovered shooting touch and the veracity of his prediction.

"You made me look like I know what I'm talking about," I told him. "I wrote about how you said you were getting ready to go off, and you do."

Gray, bouncing the basketball, was quick with his reply.

"Well that's what it's all about Dan—making you look good."

Buzz Meets His Match

So what's the lifespan of a Yellow Jacket?

The question was raised on February 22, 2004, when a yellow blur passed in front of press row at Georgia Tech's Alexander Memorial Coliseum. Buzz, the Yellow Jackets' costumed mascot, was running for his life.

For in hot pursuit was Debra Williams, the mother and steadfast supporter of Eric Williams, Wake Forest's 6-9, 275 pound center.

Buzz, perhaps the ACC's most mischievous mascot, had swiped Debra Williams's trademark yellow fedora off her head and was racing for the Georgia Tech's student section. How alarmed Buzz must have been, then, to reach the supposed sanctuary, only to see Mrs. Williams—a former basketball player herself who once pulled down 31 rebounds in a game while playing for Livingstone—wade through the crowd after him.

While the tussle ensued, Eric Williams was down on the court making a key basket in the Deacons' clutch 80-76 victory. Later Williams was cracking up over the accounts of his mother's fracas with Buzz.

"Everybody told me she had him in a headlock," Williams laughed.

It was a winning night all around for Wake Forest. While the Deacons were putting the finishing touches on one of their most impressive victories of the season, Debra Williams emerged from the student section waving the fedora above her head in triumph.

The Wake Forest fans sitting behind the Deacons' bench cheered her successful recovery. Moments later, a disheveled and dazed Buzz stumbled from the student section.

Nobody's Fool

A famous cliché among college coaches is that by tournament time, there are no more freshmen.

Once he saw his teammate Paul board the bus for the trip to Raleigh and the first and second rounds of the 2004 NCAA Tournament, Gray knew better.

For there was Paul, the point guard and emerging leader of the Deacons, walking around with a video camera.

"It's kind of funny because this morning we came in and we had a little walk-through before we get on the bus," Gray related. "Chris has a video camera. I'm like, 'What are you bringing the video camera for?'

"He said, 'I'm going to the tournament.' I'm like, 'It's not vacation buddy.'"

Prosser had a similar reaction.

"I told him it's not the senior trip to the state fair," Prosser said.

Thanks largely to the play of Paul, the Deacons also earned a trip the next week to East Rutherford, N.J. for Wake Forest's first appearance in the Sweet 16 since Tim Duncan's junior season of 1996. Paul, in two games against Virginia Commonwealth and Manhattan, had 41 points, 13 assists, 11 rebounds and only three turnovers.

Asked if he would be taking his video camera to East Rutherford, Paul proved he was nobody's fool.

"I think this time I'm going to leave it at home, because Coach let me know this is a business trip," Paul said.

When Worlds Collide

You can take the player out of Wake Forest, but as Dr. Kenneth C. Herbst proved, you can't take Wake Forest out of the player.

Herbst was a walk-on basketball player at Wake Forest from 1994 through 1997 whose greatest claim to fame was he at times roomed with Tim Duncan on the road. His only other legacy was the eight points he scored in 18 career games.

"They liked when I got into the game because it meant we were blowing out the other team," Herbst said.

So imagine the conflict Herbst felt seven years after his career when Wake Forest met St. Joseph's in the semifinal of the 2004 East Rutherford Regional. Herbst at the time was teaching at St. Joseph's as a 29-year-old assistant professor in food marketing.

Coach Phil Martelli of the Hawks often squired recruits to Herbst to have Herbst wax on the wonderful educational opportunity provided by St. Joseph's.

"My two worlds are colliding," Herbst told the media before the Deacons game against the Hawks. "No way in hell did I ever imagine the two schools I love would be playing each other in such a big game."

Herbst was pressed by a writer with the *Philadelphia Inquirer* as to which team he wanted to win.

"My entire life has been Wake Forest, Wake Forest," Herbst replied. "My heart is with the Deacs. But put it this way, if Wake has to lose, I'd rather it be to St. Joe's than any other school."

Martelli's Master Plot

After simmering, apparently for decades, the rivalry between Wake Forest and St. Joe's boiled over again in March of 2004, when the two schools played each other in the semifinals of the East Rutherford Regional.

The fire that had blazed during the 17 times the schools played each other from 1939 through 1982 was stoked by two fiery individuals, Billy Packer and Martelli.

In the days leading up to the 2004 regional semifinal, the media was abuzz over the feud between the two. It began when Packer, in his capacity as a CBS analyst, said the Hawks, despite their 27-1 regular-season record, didn't deserve a No. 1 seed in the East Rutherford Regional because of their less-than-grueling schedule.

Martelli, the coach of St. Joe's, responded tartly, calling Packer a "jackass" and wondering, "Is Billy Packer playing for a team?" Packer answered back, saying that Martelli "needs to learn a little history about the school where he coaches."

A day later, Martelli revealed he was indeed aware of Packer's heroics against St. Joe's during his playing days at Wake Forest. The Hawks led the Deacons by six points in the semifinals of the 1962 East Regional before Wake Forest rallied to tie the game and win 96-85 in overtime.

He said he was still holding a grudge against Packer, who made two baskets in the final 10 seconds of regulation to overtake the Hawks.

"The only thing about his playing career was in Cole Field House, St. Joe's was up four with 10 seconds left when he played," Martelli said. "We missed a foul shot. He came down and got a layup. Then they stole the inbounds play and he got a layup to tie the game and we lost to them in overtime.

"We don't easily forget 40 years ago, those losses."

But even in backing away from the controversy, Martelli stepped on Packer's feat. Media accounts from the game described the two shots by Packer as jump shots. The shot that tied the game was described as a 30-footer, a distance that even Packer disputed years later.

"I probably couldn't reach the basket from 30 feet," Packer said. "It's kind of like fish stories. It would have probably been a three-pointer in this day and age."

But Packer couldn't resist one more shot at St. Joe's.

"Then why wasn't St. Joe's defending a slow, fat, bald-headed Polish kid?" Packer said.

The two eventually made nice. Martelli walked over during the Hawks' practice at Continental Airlines Arena the day before the game, and offered his hand to Packer. Packer readily accepted.

One Hawk player, Tyrone Barley, practically rolled his eyes over the whole brouhaha.

"To be honest, I don't know if the players knew who Billy Packer was." Barley said. "I really didn't know who Billy Packer was.

"Everybody is entitled to their own opinion. We really didn't think too much of it. I think it was just Martelli's master plot to get more media attention."

"Just the Beginning"

In his typical self-deprecating manner, Prosser is fond of saying that even when he played basketball he couldn't play basketball.

Though he attended the U.S. Merchant Marine Academy on a basketball scholarship, he hardly had NBA scouts flocking to Kings Point, N.Y. Truth be told, he rarely escaped the bench.

"It's funny, they gave me a distinguished alumnus award two years ago," Prosser said in the spring of 2004. "They gave me my game-by-game scoring totals.

"I found out I only missed 1,000 points by 848."

Suffice it to say that Prosser, as a player, was no Chris Paul. But as a coach he quickly developed the ability to recognize the greatness in others that he lacked in himself.

And when he saw Paul playing for West Forsyth High, a school located across town in Winston-Salem from Wake Forest, Prosser knew he wanted to see Paul dressed in the Deacons' black and gold.

Other schools, obviously, coveted Paul as well. Prosser said his recruiting pitch to Paul was straight and to the point.

Prosser told Paul he wanted him to play at Wake Forest, but he wouldn't pester him about it.

"Right now you should be more concerned with winning the state championship for West Forsyth than whether Skip Prosser is at your games or at your practices," Prosser recalled.

Prosser told Paul he wasn't going to tell him he was "the greatest thing since Cheerios."

Prosser told Paul he couldn't find a better place than Wake Forest.

"I think he appreciated the honesty," Prosser said.

By late spring, Prosser had Paul over to his house. There he asked Paul, point-blank, if he was coming to Wake Forest.

Paul responded that yes, he was coming to Wake Forest, but he first wanted to visit a couple of other schools.

Prosser told him that, in that case, Wake Forest would have to start recruiting other point guards. He also told Paul that if he were, indeed, intent on coming to Wake Forest, additional visits wouldn't be fair to the other schools.

"He called me the next morning and said, 'Coach I'm not looking at anyplace else, I want to come to Wake.'" Prosser said.

The rest was history, as well as the immediate future of Wake Forest basketball. Paul, as a freshman, was ACC Rookie of the Year and led the Deacons to their first appearance in the Sweet 16 since 1996.

"He couldn't have had a better freshman year, as a player, as a person, academically," Prosser said. "You couldn't have written the script any better.

"Our goal is to make that just the beginning of what we're trying to do."

Epilogue

As small as Wake Forest University has remained over the years, the entire undergraduate student body of 3,950 would have to take turns watching a game of basketball played in Gore Gymnasium. I know this to be true, because that's where I'm sitting as I apply the finishing touches to this year-long project that I consider, above all else, a heartfelt tribute to Wake Forest basketball.

I never imagined the place would be so tiny, and I've always had a pretty lively imagination.

For instance, I can easily imagine excited fans filing in out of the raw winter's night, through the lobby and past the popcorn machines filling the arena with that enticing aroma. I can vividly imagine Coach Murray Greason sitting with his arms crossed on the bench just beyond the baseline while his assistant, Bones McKinney, twitched and jerked alongside in a spasm of nervous energy. I can imagine Dickie Hemric going up for a rebound, bowling over opponents and teammates alike in his relentless pursuit of the ball. I can certainly imagine the fire marshals looking the other way, in, as they were, on the running joke that only 2,200 were supposed to be in Gore Gym at the same time.

For months I'd been trying to make my way back through history to Gore. I'd been told it's still here, where it has been since the doors first opened in the spring of 1935, 69 years ago. Finally, today, on the kind of a brilliant and soft spring day that makes North Carolina the paradise it is, I found time to drive east from Winston-Salem, up Interstate I-40 to the new beltway around north Raleigh, and on up U.S. 1 into the leafy little town of Wake Forest.

Once in town, I followed Main Street until I reached a dead end. There, across the road, were the stately red brick buildings of the Southeastern Baptist Theological Seminary, the college that moved in when Wake Forest College moved out in 1956, to be relocated in Winston-Salem 110 miles to the west.

A friendly woman named Melody at the visitors' desk said she had never heard of Gore Gym. Shown a smoky photograph from decades past, she said it looked a great deal like the Ledford Student Center. Walking through the intimate campus and across Wingate Street, I could tell she was right. This had to be the place.

There are the wide, white concrete steps where Greason was known to fall asleep, surrounded by his precious pack of beagles. There is the small circular window above the front door.

Inside the gym, there are the arched windows, five to a side. There's the peaked wooden roof, and the steal beams off which the lantern lights hang down. Ten less than giant steps carried me from the sidelines to the brick walls on either side of the court. Thirty feet, max.

And to think, college basketball was once played here. Heroes were made and hearts were broken. Sweat was spilled on the hardwood, along with an occasional drop or two of blood. The times, and even the game, were different, but the passions were the same.

My best guess is that we don't ever outgrow our past. It remains a part of us, sometimes the best part, but always a significant part. The Jim Wallers and Herb Clines and Dickie Hemrics and Maurice Georges and Lefty Davises and Jack Williamses of those days wanted to win games and championships just as badly as the Chris Pauls and Justin Grays and Jamaal Levys and Taron Downeys and Eric Williamses of today.

When ground was broken for the new campus on October 15, 1951, President Harry Truman was on hand to give a speech. A passage of that speech is as follows:

"When the accounts of history are rendered, it is the going forward that constitutes the record."

Wake Forest basketball is indeed going forward, at an accelerated rate of speed. The record reveals that the future has never looked brighter. One day, perhaps one day soon, the Deacons will return to the Final Four. Once there, they may even win the ultimate prize, the National Championship.

And should Wake Forest ever win it all, it would behoove the university, once all the fanfare has died down in Winston-Salem, to return to the town of Wake Forest for a special ceremony at center court here at Gore Gym.

Wake Forest owes it to the past, and Wake Forest owes it to the future.

But mostly, Wake Forest owes it to itself.

—Dan Collins

Celebrate the Heroes of North Carolina Sports
and College Basketball in These Other 2004 Releases from Sports Publishing!

Tales from the Carolina Panthers Sideline
by Scott Fowler

• 5.5 x 8.25 hardcover
• 200 pages
• photos throughout
• $19.95

Dale Brown's Memoirs from LSU Basketball
by Dale Brown with Sam King

• 6 x 9 hardcover
• 200 pages
• photos throughout
• $19.95

Digger Phelps's Tales from the Notre Dame Hardwood
by Digger Phelps
with Tim Bourret

• 5.5 x 8.25 hardcover
• 200+ pages
• 30 photos throughout
• $19.95

The Indiana University Basketball Encyclopedia
by Jason Hiner

• 8.5 x 11 hardcover
• 250+ photos throughout
• color panoramic foldout
• 500+ pages • $49.95

Tales from the 1980 Louisville Cardinals
by Jim Terhune

• 5.5 x 8.25 hardcover
• 200 pages
• 25-30 photos throughout
• $19.95

Lowe's Motor Speedway: A Weekend at the Track
by Kathy Persinger

• 8.5 x 11 hardcover • 128 pages
• color photos throughout
• Includes CDracecard!
• $24.95 • (2003 release)

100 Years of Duke Basketball: A Legacy of Achievement
by Bill Brill

• 9 x 12 hardcover
• 140 photos throughout
• 240+ pages • $29.95

Beware of the Phog: 50 Years of Allen Fieldhouse
by Doug Vance and Jeff Bollig

• 9 x 12 hardcover
• 160+ pages
• 140 color photos throughout
• $29.95

Legends of N.C. State Basketball
by Tim Peeler

• 8.5 x 11 hardcover
• 144 pages
• photos throughout
• $24.95

Legends of Maryland Basketball
by Dave Ungrady

• 8.5 x 11 hardcover
• 160+ pages
• color photos throughout
• $24.95